The Ten Students

You'll Meet in Your

Classroom

The Ten Students

You'll Meet in Your

Classroom

Classroom
Management
Tips for
Middle and
High School
Teachers

Vickie Gill

CORWIN PRESS
A SAGE Publications Company
Thousand Oaks, CA 91320

For information:

Corwin Press
A Sage Publications Company
2455 Teller Road
Thousand Oaks, California 91320
www.corwinpress.com

Sage Publications Ltd.
1 Oliver's Yard
55 City Road
London EC1Y 1SP
United Kingdom

Sage Publications India Pvt. Ltd.
B 1/I 1 Mohan Cooperative Industrial Area
Mathura Road, New Delhi 110 044
India

Sage Publications Asia-Pacific Pte. Ltd.
33 Pekin Street #02-01
Far East Square
Singapore 048763

Printed in the United States of America

Library of Congress Cataloging-in-Publication Data

Gill, Vickie.
The ten students you'll meet in your classroom: Classroom management tips for middle and high school teachers / Vickie Gill.
    p. cm.
Includes bibliographical references and index.
ISBN 978-1-4129-4911-8 (cloth)—ISBN 978-1-4129-4912-5 (pbk.)
    1. Classroom management. 2. Middle school teaching. 3. High school teaching. I. Title.
LB3013.G53 2007
373.1102'4—dc22

                                    2006103450

This book is printed on acid-free paper.

07   08   09   10   11   10   9   8   7   6   5   4   3   2   1

Acquisitions Editor:	Rachel Livsey
Editorial Assistant:	Phyllis Capello
Production Editor:	Libby Larson
Copy Editor:	Jacqueline Tasch
Typesetter:	C&M Digitals (P) Ltd.
Proofreader:	Dorothy Hoffman
Cover Designer:	Scott Van Atta
Graphic Designer:	Lisa Miller

Grateful acknowledgment is made for permission to reprint excerpts from the following copyrighted works:

Page 14–"Growin' Up" by Bruce Springsteen. Copyright © 1972 Bruce Springsteen, renewed © 2000 Bruce Springste (ASCAP). Reprinted by permission. International copyright secured. All rights reserved.
Page 38–"Glory Days" by Bruce Springsteen. Copyright © 1984 Bruce Springsteen. Reprinted by permissi International copyright secured. All rights reserved.
Page 68–"Hungry Heart" by Bruce Springsteen. Copyright © 1980 Bruce Springsteen. Reprinted by permissi International copyright secured. All rights reserved.
Page 106–"Badlands" by Bruce Springsteen. Copyright © 1978 Bruce Springsteen. Reprinted by permissi International copyright secured. All rights reserved.

Contents

Chapter 1—The Good Kids   2

The vast majority of any school population is made up of good kids. These students are in school to receive the best education available, but often their teacher's time and attention are dissipated because the instructor is dealing with the discipline problems created by the minority described in the other nine groups. When not given their due, some Good Kids can themselves become negative forces in the classroom.

Chapter 2—The Rebels   14

These students can be a teacher's nightmare. Many don't want to be in school, are aggressively uninterested in what you are teaching, and are frustratingly unimpressed with whatever punishment you throw their way. They hate rules, so it's important to convince them that rules are essential components in any human interactions and that your rules are consistent, logical, and fairly enforced.

Chapter 3—The Misfits   26

Most schools are made up of an elaborate system of student cliques. Students need to belong, to be accepted, and those who cannot breach the walls surrounding The Skaters or The Jocks or The Politicians will move through the school as Misfits. If they're lucky, they'll bond with other Misfits; if not, they'll spend most of their school years resentful of their alienation.

These students are the "beautiful people"—often the most popular kids in school. Some are the star athletes, some come from wealthy families, and some are just incredibly attractive. They often give the impression that they run the school, and they do wield significant power in and outside of the classroom.

Manipulators are often hard to spot and can cause great damage to a classroom environment long before they are recognized. They are all about power and are rather clever about how to wrest control from the teacher. They will sometimes cause problems between some of the other students just to enjoy the show.

These are the kids who are fodder for the more powerful students. Sometimes, because of their size or age, they have a hard time protecting themselves. Sometimes, because of the family dynamics in which they were raised, they bring on the victim role themselves. These kids often latch on to a sympathetic teacher and, in trying to help, the teacher can actually become an enabler.

These kids can have severe learning disabilities or be so highly intelligent that they cannot relate to their peers. Some have endured extraordinary events in their lives. What marks them is that they are different, and depending on their motivations, they can be highly stimulating to teach or a severe drain on the teacher's energy and resources. Regardless, most will require a teacher who is willing to be their advocate.

The students in this group have been hurt by life. Some were horribly abused as children, physically and mentally, and hide behind their scars like a shield. They are often overtly angry or sullen and can be very frustrating to deal with in the classroom. They must be approached with caution, but they also must learn how to manage their anger.

Chapter 9—The Invisibles **106**

Every school has students who are expert at blending into the background. They quietly go about their business hoping to avoid unwanted attention from teachers and other students. Some are painfully shy; others feel like outsiders and do not know how to fit in. If they never feel a sense of connection to the community, these kids can cause incredible damage to themselves or to the school.

Chapter 10—The Perfectionists **116**

These students put themselves under tremendous pressure to be the best. They're the ones who develop ulcers from worrying and who obsessively calculate and recalculate their grade point average. They can become behavior problems if they think they can challenge the teacher's methods or system of assessment—and their parents will back them fully in this attack.

Introduction: Before You Begin . . .

I have but one lamp by which my feet are guided, and that
is the lamp of experience. I know of no way of judging of the
future but by the past.

—PATRICK HENRY

One of my favorite things about teaching is that my job is never the same. I teach high school English, and although the objectives rarely vary (to improve the reading, writing, and thinking skills of my students), I can choose from an ever-expanding list of books and topics to create my lessons. But in truth, the reason I am drawn to this profession is the students. Each year, I stand in front of a classroom full of new faces— some who smile and say "Hi" when they walk in, eager to please and be pleased, and some who slouch in at the last minute, slump in a seat in the back, and defy me to teach them anything. I find this exciting. In fact, as I scan their faces before I start "the show," I get the same tingling of anticipation I feel when I walk into a well-stocked bookstore. Every kid is a story I cannot wait to read.

When I work with my students on reading comprehension, one of the skills I try to help them develop is the ability to draw on prior knowledge before tackling a text. I tell them that I approach a research article and a gothic novel with very different mind-sets. Because I have past experience with both types of writing, I am familiar with the genres and understand how to get what I'm looking for from each. I adjust my reading speed, my attention to detail, and even my surroundings based on what has worked in the past. I don't believe that one form of writing is superior to another just because one may require more effort than the other—it's my motivation that differs. For the research article, I need to sit in a not-too-comfortable chair with plenty of light early in the day. For the gothic novel, soft music and a cup of tea in the evening will work just fine.

Like books, no two students are the same. Each is a unique individual, but because I've had the privilege of getting to know so many over my 27 years of teaching, even a kid I'm meeting for the first time will seem vaguely familiar. Every year, I spend a few weeks studying mythology with my students, partly because the stories are entertaining, but mainly because they help us to understand human nature, offer explanations for the mysteries of life, and illustrate how certain choices can invite either tragedy or triumph. I have done what I can to disguise the identity of the students I describe in this book—all of the names have been changed, yet every story is based on an actual event. But because I've taught for such a long time, each student described in this book also represents hundreds of students I've known—they have become the archetypes I draw on to help my students get over the roadblocks that life has placed in their paths. I also tell these stories in workshops when I try to help teachers understand the often baffling behavior of some of their most challenging students.

When you glance at the titles of these chapters, it's important to remember that most students can cross over into several categories. As an adolescent, I could have been called a Rebel, a Misfit, or a "Good" Kid; and depending on the class, the teacher, or whichever phase of teenage angst I was currently wallowing in, they could all have been right. Students should never be reduced to stereotypes—they are far too dynamic and complex for that. However, I have noticed that recognizing and understanding general patterns of behavior can be useful as new and experienced teachers develop specific techniques to deal effectively with discipline problems in the classroom.

I begin this book with the "Good" Kids, and that's where I start when I face a new group of students each year—they're all good kids, but I cannot be so naïve as to think that they come to me without a past, a tabula rasa, if you will. A class is not a concrete unit but a room full of individuals who may have to be reached in different ways. My experience has taught me that there are some specific, practical things I can do before school starts to eliminate 80% of the discipline problems I've encountered in my career. Tackling the other 20% requires more of a philosophical approach—a frame of mind that will help you keep your eye on the big picture, which is that we all have a basic need to be accepted and feel like we belong.

If you enter a classroom with a solid knowledge of the subject matter, a sense of humor, and some common sense, all of the rest is just details. This book contains affectionate descriptions of various kids I've taught, coupled with practical advice on how to create a classroom management plan that will allow you to spend more of your time on the job of teaching and less on dealing with discipline problems. At the end of each chapter, I have supplemented these real-life stories with a list of tips for putting these techniques into practice and samples of handouts and worksheets I use every year with my own students.

I have been a teacher for most of my life. In one of my favorite poems, Langston Hughes writes, "I've known rivers . . . My soul has grown deep like the rivers." Well, I have known students, and my life has been enriched by their stories. Let me tell you what I know.

❧ **Acknowledgments** ❧

I am blessed to be surrounded by unfailingly supportive family and friends. I would like to thank especially my daughter, Jenny Gill, and Kam Jacoby for their thoughtful comments on the text, and Delaney, Casey, Cornelia, Cynthia, Barbara, and Susie for allowing me to use them as sounding boards throughout the process. I am indebted to my editor, Rachel Livsey, for her gentle encouragement and patience. Most of all, I thank my students for sharing their stories—you honor and delight me.

The contributions of the following reviewers are gratefully acknowledged:

Jennifer Abrams, Professional Developer
Palo Alto Unified School District, Palo Alto, CA

Karen Harvey, New Teacher Program Coordinator
Santa Clarita Valley Consortium, Santa Clarita, CA

Becky Cooke, Principal
Evergreen Elementary School, Mead School District, Spokane, WA

Lori Grossman, Instructional Coordinator
ABRAZO New Teacher Induction Program, Professional Development
    Services
Houston Independent School District, Houston, TX

Tracy Carbone, Reading Recovery Teacher
Indian Trail Elementary, Indian Trail, NC

Diane Payne, Broughton High School (retired)
Raleigh, NC

Ronetta P. Wards, District Instructional Technology Coordinator
Duval County Public Schools, Jacksonville, FL

Lisa Suhr, Fourth-Grade Teacher
Sabetha Elementary School, Sabetha, KS

Melanie J. Mares, Sixth-Grade Language Arts Teacher
Team Leader, Lowndes Middle School, Valdosta, GA

Lacey Robinson, Early Childhood Content Specialist
Montgomery County Schools, Montgomery, MD

Brenda Vatthauer, Middle School Instructor
Thief River Falls Schools, Thief River Falls, MN

Joseph Staub, Resource Specialist Teacher
Thomas Starr King Middle School, Los Angeles, CA

About the Photographs

I was inspired to write this book after seeing a show of Kam Jacoby's photographs in Los Angeles. Kam teaches photography at the school where I work, and I loved looking at the expressions on the faces of these students I'd come to know so well. One of the sweetest girls struck a pose of defiance, and a young woman who is a force of nature fell into the victim stance—Kam gave them no instructions, just asked permission to take their pictures. As I listened to the people who were viewing the photographs comment on the beauty of the compositions and the intriguing expressions he had captured in the kids' faces, I had to fight the urge to interrupt by saying, "Oh, let me tell you this girl's story—it's fascinating." Now I have the chance, but it's important to say that the photos were placed randomly throughout this book. None of them necessarily match the students actually described in the chapters they illustrate. In asking for permission to use these images, the students without exception were thrilled, even when I said that some of the chapters describe rather negative behaviors. The kids loved having the attention paid and wanted people to understand and think about them as complex individuals.

In describing the photographs in an artist's statement, Kam writes:

These portraits of teenagers were taken at the high school where I have been teaching since 1998. I photographed the students during breaks between classes or on their lunch hour. These are guarded, yet revealing portraits of an unusual cross-section of teenagers. They are individuals on the brink of adulthood, perhaps not fully formed, but with the shadows of experience beginning to show in their faces.

I didn't pose the students, but that is not to say that they are unposed photographs. They are certainly responding, consciously or unconsciously, to the images with which they are inundated on an hourly basis. They have been photographed enough to know what they look like, and they position themselves in front of the camera, altering their countenance to match a collective memory of the latest unsmiling model selling image, sexuality, and acceptance. The clothes that they wear and their facial expressions hide the insecurities, the doubts, and the self-consciousness of adolescents. At their best, the portraits allow a glimpse into the persona hiding behind the mask.

About the Author

Photo by Kam Jacoby

Vickie Gill is an award-winning teacher who has taught high school English, remedial reading, and journalism in both California and Tennessee. She is the author of two books published by Corwin Press, including *The Eleven Commandments of Good Teaching* and *The Ten Commandments of Professionalism in Teaching.* Contact her at vgill@juno.com to set up workshops for your school system or to discuss the ideas presented in this book.

About the Photographer

Kam Jacoby has been a photography teacher for the last 15 years, on both the high school and college levels. His work has been exhibited throughout the United States. For more information about the photographs in this book, write to him at kamjac@hotmail.com.

CHAPTER 1

The Good Kids

The tendency of man's nature to good is like the tendency of water to flow downward.

—MENG-TSE

The overwhelming majority of the kids in school are what teachers often describe as "the Good Kids." This phrase is used in sentences like, "I want that boy out of my class because he's ruining it for the Good Kids." These are the students who show up to school every day generally knowing what is expected of them. Most of these kids have goals and recognize school as a necessary step toward preparing for their futures. They cause little trouble in your classroom, are willing to help you and their peers, and go home to families who actively encourage them to do well in school. The Good Kids are in school to receive the best education available, but often, your time and attention are dissipated because you are dealing with the discipline problems created by a few chronically disruptive students. If you create a negative atmosphere in trying to control the class, some of these Good Kids can themselves become behavior problems.

✑ **Creating a Sense of Community** ✑

I believe that every child starts out as a Good Kid, but outside forces can change the way children feel about themselves and the people in their lives, especially the authority figures. Every year, I open my classroom door to greet smiling, confident faces, students who may not be thrilled to be back in school but who are willing to give me a chance. But mixed into this group are a few kids who ignore me as they chatter with their friends, refuse to look me in the eye, or glare in defiance—I know I have to catch them right away. I spend a great deal of time in the first week creating a sense of community, generating excitement for the curriculum, and setting up the classroom expectations. My two goals are to make sure that every student feels known and that every student understands what will cause a problem and how I'll react to that problem. My mind-set is that all of them are good, and I want to keep them that way.

Gathering the Basic Information

This is what I do at the beginning of every school year. Before the kids arrive, I ask a counselor or registrar to let me know which students are called by names different from those printed on the roll sheet. For example, some students go by their middle names or shorten Rebecca to Becca. I endeared myself to one feisty young man in Tennessee by calling him Cooter instead of Herbert when I first took roll. I'd never met him and was advised to use Cooter by another teacher, and this gave the boy a sense that I knew him on the first day of class. Then, I watch carefully as the students come into the room and make a point to memorize the names of the noisier students as quickly as possible. I don't assign my students to a seating chart, but I make a quick sketch of where they sit because they will often go to the same seats on the next day. I use the sketch to call roll instead of my computer list, so I can learn their names by the end of the week. Later in the year, I may give assigned seating to two or three students who work better on opposite sides of the room, but I don't like the idea of taking away the choice of where to sit from the Good Kids. However, I've also known outstanding teachers who are very strict about where students can sit at the beginning of the school year so that they can offer the privilege of seating choice as a reward for good behavior later on. It is true that it's easier to ease up rather than tighten the reins, but I find I work better in a more relaxed atmosphere—I'm trying to create a classroom that I would have looked forward to joining when I was a kid.

Opening-day classes are often shorter, which allows the kids to move through their entire schedule or attend a welcoming assembly, so I generally just introduce the curriculum and myself, then distribute the syllabus and course description. I also have them fill out a form that includes their parent contact information, their birth dates (I like to acknowledge birthdays throughout the year, even for high school kids), and a few questions that will give me a general sense of what they feel they need to learn (a copy of the Information Sheet is included at the end of this chapter).

In the beginning of each school year, my students walk into a room with blank walls. For homework on the first day, I ask them to bring in their favorite quotes—words of wisdom that have inspired them over the years. At the end of the week, I give them colorful 8 x 24-inch rectangles of poster board and ask them to write down their quotes and pin them to the wall. The last class of the day is stunned by the transformation in the room—words and colors everywhere—and they are anxious to contribute their truths to the walls. These quotes are often the first real insight I have into how my students view the world. I add a couple of my favorites and refer to these often as I teach, and many students incorporate each other's sayings into the essays they write throughout the year.

Testing the Rules

From the second day to the fifth day, I go over the rules and consequences—a little each day. I start by handing out the contract and explaining what I expect—I tell them they'll have a quiz on the class rules at the end of the week so that I can be sure everyone understands exactly what to do (a copy of the rules and the quiz are included at the end of Chapter 2). I predict that everyone will do well on the quiz and make sure that's true by practicing the rules with them for a few minutes every day. Sometimes I shoot out questions: "What happens the first time you're late to class?" "What happens if you ignore a verbal warning?" I act amazed when a number of them know the answers and restate my confidence in the fact that they'll all be ready for the quiz by the end of the week. Other times I ask, "What do I mean by 'Don't disturb other people?'" and I act that out. I try to be funny and supportive and light-hearted—the general impression I want to leave with them is that I am confident that they all want to go along with my expectations because it will create an environment where I can help them achieve their goals. I also want them to understand specifically how to conduct themselves in my class and specifically what will happen if they ignore these rules.

✑ Causing Good Kids to Go Bad ✑

The Good Kids enter your classroom more or less willing to participate and follow your directions. They have a great deal of tolerance for teachers who are not engaging or skilled at classroom management. They will often sit silently when a problem erupts and wait for the lesson to begin again. Some of them are used to being in classes where a power play between a teacher and a student will eat up a significant amount of the class time, so they bring books to read or just quietly begin their homework. Usually, these kids will not cause a problem themselves unless the teacher botches the behavior management so badly that the Good Kids feel compelled to defend the troublemakers.

We teachers need to be careful to criticize a student's action and not a student's character. Most kids have heard quite a few lectures about their faults and shortcomings long before they ever enter your room, and the worst-behaved kids have heard these criticisms so often that they have developed defense mechanisms that you can easily trigger. Some of the most difficult students have huge egos and little self-confidence, so deciding to verbally knock them down a few pegs can backfire and turn the entire class against you. When the second of my three daughters was in high school, her teachers would have described her as a Good Kid, but she—this girl who never broke a school rule in her life—voluntarily participated in a prank to get back at a particularly strict teacher who tried to control his students with an iron fist. When he left his classroom for a few minutes to take a student to the office, the entire class jumped up and turned all of the pictures in the room upside down. The teacher would have been wise to laugh at the prank and move on, but this teacher blew up and spent a ridiculous amount of time trying to get the guilty to confess, which of course no one did. My daughter told me later that she thought the prank was fun and that she was not impressed by the teacher's angry response because "he yells at everyone all of the time anyway." If you think about it, all teachers create a sense of community in their classrooms. The ideal is for you and your students to bond in reaching a common productive goal, but in this case, the teacher foolishly created a community that did nothing more than unite all of the students in their disdain for him.

Another mistake you can make with the Good Kids is to use them as examples for proper behavior when disciplining another student—the old "Why can't you be more like Susie?" Both the troublemaker and the Good Kid will resent this comparison and distance themselves from you for resorting to such a weak defense. Good Kids also tell me that they resent being paired in group work with students who are discipline problems because the teacher hopes the Good Kid will somehow manage the behavior of his or her peer. This can happen, but breaking kids into groups should appear random, and the groups should change often.

Relying on Common Sense

Possibly the main characteristic that separates the Good Kids from those who continually cause problems in the classroom is that the Good Kids rely on their common sense more often. I actually spend some time talking to my students about developing fine-tuned "crap detectors" (I make it very clear that "crap" refers to nonsense). This is a little light that goes on inside your head when you see or hear something that isn't true or makes little sense. Mine goes off when I watch commercials on TV or when I hear a teacher or a parent tell a kid to "Do it because I say so." I would never dream of calling a student a liar when he's giving me the 15 reasons why he doesn't have his homework, none of which include that he forgot or didn't do it. Instead, at around Excuse No. 8, I grab my ear and say, "Beep, beep, beep—I'm sorry, I can't hear you—my crap detector is going off." The kid and the class usually laugh, and the situation is quickly defused.

You can cause your students' crap detectors to go off by choosing the wrong battles to fight. I have seen huge arguments erupt in a classroom over whether or not a student needs to use the restroom—trust me, you'll lose this one. Some of the girls take great delight in challenging a male teacher with "female problems," and I've seen a dramatic performance worthy of an Academy Award put on by a kid who "can't hold it anymore!" It's best to let them go, but with a system based on common sense. I tell my students they have one emergency to leave the room every class period, but they must follow the guidelines I've set under the rule, "Don't disturb other students." If they must leave the room to go to the bathroom, they are to exit and enter again quietly so that they do nothing to draw attention to themselves (I actually demonstrate how to do this). Also, they may be gone for only a few minutes—if it's too long, I'll worry that there is something wrong and have to look for them. Finally, they are responsible for any information they miss, and I ask them not to leave when their group is coming to the Board at the front of the class to work with me. I rarely have a problem with this, and the students appreciate the fact that I trust them. If your school has a general policy about restroom use based on the safety of the students, then you need to follow those guidelines; your students won't resent you because it's out of your hands.

There are a few other brush fires I try to avoid before they start. One, I don't allow my students to bring food or drinks to class because I have computers in the room, and I find that a kid eating a snack can be distracting. However, I do allow them to bring in bottled water because I keep a bottle of water for myself on my desk. Also, I often work with my students in groups, and I don't want to be disturbed by random questions when I'm working with a small group at the Board, so after a few weeks, I appoint a contact person for each group. This is someone who knows a bit about computers and won't mind if the students in his or her group quietly ask for help with minor problems. In addition, it's against the rules of my class to stand by the door to wait for the bell to ring (too distracting, and more behavior problems can happen in this brief time than in the rest of the period). Finally, they laugh, but when I'm getting them ready for the rules quiz, I ask the kids when it's OK to sleep in my class. They say, "Never!" and I say, "Right! (dramatic pause)—unless I'm sleeping, then feel free to snooze away." They enjoy the humor and get the point. All of the time you spend at the beginning of the year working out the details on classroom management will buy you far more time later in the year for teaching. This strategy also eliminates the impression that you're reacting to misbehavior out of anger—it simply becomes a cause/effect issue that was clearly explained before a problem occurs.

Good Kids do well in school, not necessarily because they're the brightest or most talented, but because they view the world from a rather balanced perspective. You should tap into that same pool of common sense when you plan your classroom management strategies. We have all had the experience of sitting at lunch and overhearing another teacher describe an out-of-control student in her class and we think, "but he never gives me any problems." The trick is to let your students know that you want to have them in your class (of course you do—without the students you have no job) and that your class is designed to help them reach their goals.

In the following chapters, I'll be discussing nine different types of students who can be a challenge to work with in the classroom. I use the same basic rules and consequences for all of my students, but in a few cases, I need to tweak my normal responses to find a way to approach a kid who is basically good but has learned some inappropriate coping skills that can disrupt the positive atmosphere I've tried to create in my classroom. I really do believe that "the tendency of man's nature [is] to good" and that if I can make them feel safe enough to relax their defenses, even the most difficult students will allow themselves to become positive members of the classroom community.

✎ **Classroom Management Tips** ✍

- Make sure that when your students leave your class at the end of the year, they appreciate why you are so passionate about the subject you teach.
- Avoid creating a "me against them" situation in your class.
- Never try to shame the troublemakers by comparing them to the Good Kids.
- Remember that the more time you spend practicing and reviewing the class rules at the beginning of the year, the less time you'll spend on the consequences later on. Give an assessment at the end of the first week about the rules and consequences so that you can work individually with students who don't quite understand the expectations or organization. Give them the opportunity to retake the rules quiz so that they can earn an excellent grade on this first and most important assessment.
- Get as much specific information about the students, their goals, and their perception of what they need to learn to help you plan your lessons (see example on the next page).

Information Sheet

 (please print neatly)

Name _____

Date of birth _____ e-mail address _____

Mother's name _____ e-mail address _____

Father's name _____ e-mail address _____

Other guardians _____

Home address _____

Home phone number _____

What do you like to do in your spare time? _____

What type of work would you like to do later in your life? _____

Which reading, writing, or life skills would you specifically like to work on this year?

(Put a check next to the skills that give you the most trouble):

_____ Organizing an essay_____ Creating a thesis statement

_____ Timed writing _____ Writing summaries

_____ Research papers

_____ Spelling _____ Vocabulary _____ Grammar and usage

_____ Reading comprehension (understanding what I read)

_____ Reading retention (remembering what I read)

_____ Taking notes _____ Listening _____ Public speaking

_____ Study skills

_____ Figuring out what I want to do with my life

_____ Learning how to improve my personal relationships

Anything else?_____

CHAPTER 2

The Rebels

"... when they said 'Sit down' I stood up"

—FROM THE BRUCE SPRINGSTEEN
COMPOSITION ENTITLED "GROWIN' UP"

These students are a teacher's nightmare—I've heard them called "Rebels Without a Pause." They don't want to be in school, are aggressively uninterested in what you are teaching, and are frustratingly unimpressed with whatever punishment you throw their way. I was one of these teenagers, which has turned out to be a tremendous advantage when I spot one in my class. Sometimes I'm not exactly sure what to do, but I sure know what not to do.

Creating Rules That Make Sense

I was a full-blown Rebel by the time I was in seventh grade—I had to be. I was raised in a male-dominated household with a "my way or the highway" father whose opinions and rules were not open to discussion. As the only girl among four siblings, I had two choices: disappear or learn to stand up for myself. By the time I entered junior high school, I was frustrated with the lack of control I had over anything that mattered to my life, so school became the place where I would try to wrest what power I could. If an overly critical autocrat of a teacher pushed all of the wrong buttons in me, I would spend a great deal of my time in that class devising creative means of upsetting that teacher. The worst mistake a teacher could make with me was to allow me to be anonymous—just another troublemaker. I loved sitting in the back of the class, hiding behind one of the girls with big hair, waiting for an opportunity to disrupt the lesson. I was a jerk, without a doubt—rude, obnoxious, unreachable—but in some cases, I was aping the behaviors the teachers were modeling for their students.

My poor ninth-grade English teacher, Mrs. Smith, was a nervous woman whose basic method for classroom management centered on threats and insults—there is no doubt in my mind that she was given the standard "Don't smile until Christmas" advice when she was preparing to become an educator. I never got to know her as a person, but I've often wondered why she chose teaching as a profession because the general impression most of her students had was that she hated kids. Her classroom management strategy was to take control of her class from the first day through the use of strict rules and fear. The trouble was (1) none of us was afraid of her and (2) her rules were unenforceable. The minute I spotted her list of "Classroom Don'ts" posted in the front of the room, I knew we would have an amusing session that day—at least for my classmates and me. Within the first 10 minutes, Mrs. Smith was screaming at random people to "sit down and shut up!" I knew better than to overtly defy her—by this time, I considered myself a seasoned professional and preferred more subtle methods of introducing chaos into the classroom. I waited while Mrs. Smith forcefully recited her list of rules, smiling to myself after I heard the first two. "Rule Number 1: No Talking! Rule Number 2: Do Not Get Out of Your Seat!" There were several other commands concerning hands and feet and the chewing of gum, but they weren't necessary for my plan. Mrs. Smith concluded her speech with a few vague threats as to the consequences of breaking any of these rules, but it was obvious to me that this teacher had come to class without a clear idea of what she was asking the students to do—or what she would do if they refused.

I knew that at some point, Mrs. Smith would turn her back to the class to write something on the board. That was my chance. I took the pen off my desk and tossed it on to the floor about three feet to my left. When she turned around, the first thing she saw was my desperately raised hand flailing in the air.

Mrs. Smith: (sharply) What is it!

Me: I'm sorry, Mrs. Smith, but I dropped my pen, and I can't reach it. It's against the rules for me to talk, so I can't ask Mindy to get it for me; and I can't get out of my seat, so would you please get it for me?"

Mrs. Smith was stunned and looked suspiciously at my innocent smile, but the class was watching, so she marched to the back of the room, picked up my pen, slammed it on my desk, and headed to the front again. I thanked her sweetly, then tossed the pen to the right of my desk before she reached the first row. She faced the class again, and there was my hand frantically flagging her down.

Mrs. Smith: WHAT!

Me: I'm sorry, I guess I'm just nervous because it's the first day of class and I want to do everything just right, but I dropped my pen again—it's over there, but I can't ask Joey to get it because I'm not supposed to talk, and I can't get out of my seat, so would you please. . . .

I never got to the end of the sentence.

Mrs. Smith: "COME WITH ME TO THE OFFICE, YOUNG LADY!!!"

I was already out of my seat. I'd been to the office many times in previous years, so this was nothing new. My fellow students applauded and gave me the thumbs up sign: "Way to go, Vickie, a new record!" They were most appreciative because I'd just bought them 15 minutes of teacher-free time. In their minds, the teacher got just what she deserved.

Mrs. Smith dragged me into the principal's office where he winced when he looked up and saw me, "What did you do now?"

"Oh, sir, I'm trying so hard to start out this year on the right foot, just as you suggested at the end of last year. And she has these rules, and one says don't talk, another don't get out of your seat, and I dropped my pen, and, and, and. . . . "

"Is this true, Mrs. Smith?" he asked.

Poor Mrs. Smith sputtered and fumed, but what could she say? I'd followed her rules to the letter. I'm sure I spent many hours over the next few months sitting outside of her classroom, but I didn't care. She lost me within the first few minutes of the school year, and even though English was my favorite subject, our relationship was so antagonistic that I preferred to doodle in my notebook as I sat on the floor in the hallway rather than listen to her lessons. She had no idea that I read every book on the assigned reading list, but I failed the tests on purpose. I didn't want her to think that she'd taught me anything.

No doubt, I was a jerk. I was winning lots of battles, but eventually I would lose the war. Mrs. Smith controlled the grades, and even though I was never held back a year, I ultimately paid the price by having to attend a junior college for two years to earn a grade point average (GPA) that would get me into a university. When I spot an overt

Rebel in my classroom, I'll sometimes act out this story for his or her class in the first week before there are any discipline problems. The kids find the whole sad tale amusing and horrifying, but in the end, I can make two points: (1) I wasted an incredible amount of time—mine and my classmates'—and (2) if Mrs. Smith had responded to my challenge with humor and kindness, and if she had put a little effort into trying to get to know me, she could have defused the whole situation. I doubt she ever would have been my favorite teacher—most of her students disliked her, and she quit the profession after two years—but Mrs. Smith forgot the cardinal rule of teaching: Model the behavior you would like your students to display.

One of the most difficult aspects of teaching is that it's a performance art and the kids are watching. They will learn patience, kindness, and good manners not by following rules, but by observing how we teachers react to infractions of those rules. Last year, a frustrated new math teacher reported to me that she had just told a rather obnoxious group of kids, "I'll show you the same respect you show me!" I told her that she was wrong—she needed to show them far more respect because she was their role model. These are skills to be demonstrated and practiced, just like multiplication and division. For some kids, the classroom may be the only place where they will see an adult acting in a grown-up manner.

I often tell the story of my misspent youth when I'm asked to give inservice presentations on classroom management techniques. It's become a greatest hit because it shocks and amuses the young teachers, many of whom are just a few years older than their students, and it also has the ring of truth. I ask for a show of hands to determine how many of them earned straight A's in high school—usually around 20% of the participants will raise their hands. Then I ask the "mostly A's and B's" students to raise their hands as well. With the occasional exception of one or two people, the entire group will have their hands in the air. I point out that this is why it is so difficult for them to deal with students who hate school and who cannot be threatened with bad grades. In junior high school, I used to wear my string of F's like notches on my belt. I was labeled a troublemaker early on, kind of liked the image, and didn't know how to break the stereotype. Luckily for me, my family moved when I was 15, and I had the chance to reinvent myself in the new school.

Demonstrating That Rules Are Necessary

With a Rebel, it's important to have a few logical rules that are clearly explained. I find the "why" behind the rules to be the most important part of the explanation. I tell the kids that I resent being told to do something (or not do something) when I don't see the point. I make them laugh by saying that it used to drive me nuts as a teenager when I'd ask a teacher, "Why do we have to learn this stuff?" The response was invariably, "Don't get smart with me!" to which I would respond, "I thought I was in school to get smart!" and the whole exchange would go downhill from there. We teachers should have a valid answer to that question. If you are spending a great deal of time mastering and delivering lessons in a particular subject, you should be able to demonstrate why these skills are useful. If you can't, you won't be able to sell your curriculum to the kids. In fact, when designing the syllabus for a class, that should be the starting place—why is it important and/or useful to learn this stuff?

The same goes for your classroom rules. A few years ago, a student walked into my class dressed in a Russian soldier's overcoat with various communist insignias on his collar and sleeves. This caused a bit of unease among his peers, but I just smiled at Carl and made a note when he asked to be called "Commie" instead of his given name. In introducing the curriculum, I made it very clear that I appreciated students who cared enough about their own education to ask why, prompting Commie to smile at me for the first time. I gave the students a sheet of paper that listed the five rules and the consequences of breaking the rules (a copy of this contract is printed at the end of this chapter). I very carefully explained the rules, acted out any vague phrases—for example, what it means to "disturb the class"—and offered the reasoning behind the rules. For the majority of the students, this was familiar territory, and they happily signed the contract stating that they had read and understood the rules. Commie wouldn't sign until I pointed out that signing the contract did not mean that he agreed with the rules, just that he understood them—kind of a reading comprehension clause. Before the end of class, he handed me the signed contract but muttered something about fascist dictators as he left my room.

A few weeks later, I was walking down the hallway when I noticed a leaflet taped to the front of Commie's locker. I chuckled as I read his manifesto demanding the immediate banishment of all school rules—"Is this not the land of the free!? Rules are the establishment's petty attempt to control the masses!" and so on. The boy was a writer, all right, but like poor Mrs. Smith from my ninth-grade year, he didn't really understand what he was asking. When I ran into him later that day, I told Commie that I very much enjoyed reading his manifesto. He looked surprised because he clearly saw me as part of the establishment. He asked if I'd read the whole thing, and I assured him that not only had I read it, I was delighted to have been given the invitation. He asked me hesitantly, "What invitation?"

"Well, since you don't believe in rules, I took something from your locker—no rule against that. Thanks." He just stared at me in disbelief, so I quickly reassured him, "Oh, don't worry, it's just a little thing, you won't really miss it, but it just caught my fancy—I've always wanted one. Again, thanks. Oops, there's the bell, you'd better run to your next class so you won't be late." A look of complete confusion passed over his face, and he hurried away. At the end of the day, he burst into my classroom and said that he had searched his entire locker as well as his backpack and could not find anything missing. I smiled sweetly and told him it was just something little, and he shot back, "You can't just go in my locker and take stuff!" I nodded and answered calmly, "So you do believe in rules. I didn't take anything. I just wanted to test out the manifesto because I have a bit of trouble with rules myself—interesting idea, though." This was all handled with a sense of humor and an appreciation for his intelligence.

We ended up becoming great friends in his remaining four years at the high school, and he was wise enough to appreciate the irony of the situation. I was wise enough to spot his sense of humor and intelligence from the first day he entered my class. I would never try to teach such a life lesson until the student and I had developed a positive relationship—Commie knew that I fully accepted him as he was and understood his desire to "rage against the machine."

This has become one of my favorite stories to tell as I introduce to my classes the hard fact that rules are necessary in any social interaction. I repeat this story with Commie's full permission, and it delights the emerging Rebels in my class. They see not only that I am unafraid of their unique view of the world but that I embrace their spirit. I also let them know that I have an agenda, I have rules for a reason, and I am willing to protect the agenda by applying consequences if necessary.

Rebels come in all shapes and sizes—some harder to spot than others. They can be the sweet straight-A student who gets along with her teachers as long as she is in control of the class. Others enter your room pierced and tattooed, with their angst emblazoned across their chests. Regardless, they must be handled with care. In my mind, the trick is to embrace their rebellious nature rather than fear it. Like every human trait, rebelliousness has a positive as well as a negative side. A frustrated teacher might view these students as disrespectful, cruel, misguided, annoying, egocentric little twits. But with a slight shift of the prism through which you gaze at your class, these kids can be courageous, insightful, brazenly honest, challenging—and if they feel you understand and respect them, some of your most protective devotees.

❧ **Classroom Management Tips** ❧

- Model the behavior you would like your students to display in your classroom.
- Visualize the way you want to organize your class and anticipate the behaviors that would inhibit learning.
- Physically set up your classroom to avoid problems before they get there. Spread students out as much as you can and allow for unobtrusive movement in the room.
- Generate a few logical rules that can be easily explained (see example on the next page).
- Make sure that whatever consequence you choose for breaking a rule makes sense and make sure you're willing to enforce it. Avoid empty threats.
- The students should definitely have the idea that you have rules in your class, not to achieve some false sense of power, but to simplify things and to eliminate chaos. The rules will help them as much as they help you.

❧ **Ms. Gill—English** ❧

Expectations for Classroom Behavior

Rules:	Consequences:
1. Be on time	1. One demerit (two free passes per semester)
2. Come prepared to work	2. Verbal warning, then Reflective Essay
3. Follow directions	3. Verbal warning, then Reflective Essay
4. No food or drinks in the classroom	4. Verbal warning, then Reflective Essay
5. Don't disturb other students	5. Verbal warning, then Reflective Essay

The Reflective Essay: A student who is having problems remembering the rules of the class will write a 250-word essay reflecting on the causes and effects of the infraction, as well as a plan of action for avoiding the problem in the future. The essay must be turned in at the beginning of the next class meeting.

If the essay is one day late, it will expand to 500 words. If the expanded essay is not turned in at the beginning of the next class meeting, the student will be sent to the office to meet with an administrator. The student may return to class when the essay is completed.

I have read and understand the rules and the consequences for breaking the rules in Ms. Gill's class:

Name (print) _____

Signature _____

Date _____

Name _____

Period _____

Expectations and Organization Quiz

1. How many times may you be tardy in a semester before you receive a demerit?

2. When is it OK to stand by the door to wait for the bell to ring or to sleep in class?

3. What should you bring to class every day? (three things)

4. What happens if you are more than 10 minutes late to class?

5. What happens the first time you disturb another student or the group at the Board?

6. What happens the second time you disturb another student within the same class period?

7. What should you do if you have a problem at your seat or on the computers?

8. What happens if you forget to bring in your Reflective Essay the day after it is assigned?

9. When may you have food or drinks (other than bottled water) in the classroom?

10. What should you do if you need to use the restroom during class?

CHAPTER 3

The Misfits

I was happy to outrage anybody who liked to be outraged.

—FRANK ZAPPA

Functional or not, every school is a community made up of groups who gather for a common purpose. When I was a kid, we called them cliques, and we formed our identities based on which clique would accept us. I was a Rebel partly because of my wiring and partly because that was the group that embraced me when I was entering adolescence. In many ways, I was a Misfit, too. I smoked in the bathrooms, dressed to shock, and defied authority as often as I could; but always, I knew that I was playing this role for acceptance and out of boredom—it wasn't the "real me."

Everyone needs to belong, to be accepted, and those students who cannot breach the walls surrounding the Skaters or the Jocks or the Politicians will move through the school as Misfits. If they're lucky, they'll find other Misfits with a common interest that brings out the best in them; if not, they'll spend most of their school years alone or aligned to a group of kids that feed on their common sense of alienation.

Finding the Face Behind the Mask

Misfits often dress to provoke—long before tattoos became de rigueur, these kids showed up at school with as many as they could afford. Their tattoos are not the tasteful butterfly hidden just below the waistline; Misfits have a banshee on the shoulder or a gun with a rose trailing down their calves. If some of the more rebellious students have five piercings in their ears, Misfits come to school with spikes through their noses, cheeks, and eyebrows. The trick when these kids enter your classroom is not to overreact to their appearance, yet to give them credit for the amount of work this takes. I ran into a former student—who was a classic Misfit—a year after he had graduated. He was always pushing the borders of what the school dress code would tolerate, so when he was free from school, he made up for lost time with a vengeance. He and I had a friendly relationship when he was a student in my journalism class because I looked well past his appearance, so we were glad to run into each other at the record shop where he was working. But I had to keep myself from bursting out laughing when I saw his piercings—he had enough metal in his face alone to set off every metal detector within a 20-mile radius. We hugged carefully, then I gently patted his cheek and said, "Ouch." He laughed and we spent a fine time catching up on what we'd been doing over the last year. I think it's silly to punch holes in our bodies, but I was glad that I hadn't allowed my personal prejudices about piercings to alienate him when he was a student in my class.

Many of the Misfits I've known have kept out of serious trouble by joining a band. Music becomes their savior—a place of escape with other people who have a great tolerance for the outrageous. I have a friend who was an outsider for most of his childhood because of his home life. His mother had been married eight times to alcoholic, abusive men, most of whom were in the military, so Daniel and his brothers had attended 13 different schools by the time he was 15. Daniel was extremely intelligent but stopped trying to fit in at school because he knew he'd be there for only a short while. His mother finally settled in one place when Daniel was in high school, and he fell in with a group of musicians, who offered him the first real acceptance he had ever been given in his life. His older brother developed no such talent and hung with a group of boys who spent most of the day stoned and most of the night beating up and robbing GIs as they left the bars to go back to the base. Both Daniel and his brother were Misfits, but their lives took very different paths because their identities were forged by the groups who accepted them.

Seeking Acceptance in All the Wrong Places

I've seen lonely kids bond with other lonely kids over a common love of computer gaming or skateboarding or radical politics, but the saddest group I've dealt with as a teacher involves those girls who use random sex as their ticket to acceptance. When Trisha walked into my room, the other students started snickering. She was a pretty girl but a bit overweight, with way too much black eyeliner and way too much cleavage showing. I kept an eye on Trisha over the first weeks of school and noticed that she was universally shunned by the other girls but was usually surrounded by a group of boys during the breaks and at lunch. Through her journal entries, I learned that Trisha's parents were divorced and that her older brother had chosen to live with his father while Trisha was forced to stay with her mom. She and her mother battled often and long over Trisha's poor grades, her clothes, and the fact that she stayed out too late at night. Trisha had been devastated by the split-up of her family and used that pain to stoke her mother's guilt. In the second month of the school year, I noticed that Joey—one of the school's star athletes—often gave Trisha a ride home at the end of the day. I was talking with Joey one day about various things and asked if he and Trisha were going together. He physically backed away from me and said a little too loudly, "Hell, no! She's a slut!!" I said that I noticed that they were often together after school. Joey just smirked and said, "Hey, if she's giving it away, I'll take it." I told Joey that I had a news flash for him—Trisha was a person, and his cold-blooded attitude toward her was pathetic and dangerous at the same time. He looked a little ashamed, but he told me that she was having sex with lots of different guys—everyone knew.

I tried to talk with Trisha, first in response to her journal entries, then later at lunch or after class. Her viewpoint on the whole situation was chilling and one I've heard over and over again through the years; she was "hooking up" out of boredom—it was no big deal—they call it "friends with privileges." To her, sex was no more intimate than sitting in a movie theater with someone—it was something to do. I was able to persuade Trisha to talk with the school's counselor, but it was a little too late. The other students became more open in their derision of her, her grades plummeted, and one day she just stopped coming to school. Later on, she attended continuation high school, and the last time I saw her, she was living on the streets in Oakland, California, crashing at one person's place or another. She wanted to go to an art school, but she needed to save up enough money to get in. I walked away from our brief conversation depressed that she was still a Misfit desperately searching for a place and a way to fit in.

⤷ Bringing Forth What Is Within You ⤶

My classroom is covered with my students' quotes, and I put up a few of my own favorite sayings. One I refer to often as I teach is said to have been found when they uncovered the Dead Sea Scrolls: "If you bring forth what is within you, what you bring forth will save you. If you do not bring forth what is within you, what you do not bring forth will destroy you." This quote makes me think of William. I have no idea whether Trisha found what was within her, but I know William did, and it transformed him. When he first came into my classroom, William was dressed like the musicians he most identified with—the punk bands. Every article of clothing was black, as was his hair and the liner around his eyes. He caused quite a stir because it seemed as if he was trying to provoke the rude comments that were thrown at him, but he never responded in a negative way. He was a quiet but positive member of my class and was always willing to tackle whatever assignment I dreamed up. He had good reason to be angry—his mother had died when he was 11, and his father had retreated into his own sorrow with very little strength to offer to his son. At that time, my favorite Rebel, Commie, was a senior, and he took William under his wing. Together, they worked to raise the political consciousness of the student body and became active in raising funds for various relief organizations. They and a few of their friends amused themselves by pushing the boundaries, especially as far as the dress code was concerned, but they had a positive spirit about them that did not put the administrators on the defensive. At Commie's urging, William entered the talent show, saying he was going to lip sync to a song. He stepped out on stage with a bare chest, torn black pants, chains, and military boots and proceeded to fling himself about the stage to a Death Metal song. At first, the audience was stunned and began to laugh nervously; but there was something pure about William's unself-conscious abandonment to the music, and by the end of the performance, the students and teachers were on their feet cheering. William had been completely accepted on his own terms. After Commie graduated, William became more and more involved in school activities and assumed several leadership roles. By his senior year, the faculty was in the habit of using him as a go-between when dealing with students who were hard to reach. The establishment as well as those who felt disenfranchised trusted William—he became a very important person on campus. When students share their philosophy of life with me—either in their journals or through casual conversations—I listen carefully, ask questions, then tell them I'll be watching. When they ask what that means, I reply that the test of the truths that make up your belief system is not the words you use but how that philosophy manifests itself in your life. Trisha's truths do not work, William's do—that's the bottom line.

✑ **Fitting In** ✑

One of the first pieces of advice I offer to new teachers is to build a sense of community in each of their classes—that's why I ask the kids to decorate my room with their truths. In the same way, a school needs to establish an identity as a community made up of a wide range of individuals who are valued for their differences. Misfits want to belong; those who feel shut out will find their own way in. I've known of teachers' own children who found acceptance by providing most of the drugs that were sold on campus. I've been in only one school where there was a problem with guns and knives being brought in, but I have been aware of kids like the boys at Columbine who were walking time bombs because of their status as outsiders. I've talked with many educators who are puzzled by students who embrace gangs, knowing full well that their involvement with those groups represents a death sentence. One of the reasons that I don't attack other people, resort to violence when I'm angry, or break the law is that I have too much to lose. I love my life, my home, my freedom. We teachers have to help the Misfits in our schools find something positive—like a band or dreams of the future—that becomes too important to risk. As their teachers, we can be the source of that inspiration by listening with interest to their points of view and by exposing them to ideas and experiences that will help them create a vision of themselves at their best.

Classroom Management Tips

- In dealing with your students, find and celebrate the unique individual behind the mask. Help the kids create a concrete vision of themselves at their very best—some people go through their whole lives without ever figuring out what that looks like.
- Help your students understand that prejudice is always based in fear, and be conscious of that yourself if you are offended by the way a Misfit is dressed.
- Sponsor a Day of Tolerance in your school to expose students and faculty to lifestyles and beliefs that may be very different from their own.
- Be tolerant when a Misfit brushes up against the borders of the school rules. Don't rescind the rules—that would take away all of the fun of rebelling—but let the students dress as they choose within the realm of common sense.
- Find a way to create a sense of community in your classroom that makes every student feel like an important member of that group. On the next two pages, I've included handouts from an activity I do with my students in the first week of school. It takes the place of the standard "Peer Interview" activity often used to help kids get to know each other. On the first day of class, I ask the students to write down the names of everyone in the room whom they know well. I use this list the next day to create pairs of students who are casual acquaintances or complete strangers and ask them to make certain low-risk assumptions about each other. First, the students look at their partners and in 8 minutes write down a series of assumptions. Next, the partners get together and quietly share their assumptions for 10 minutes, correcting any that are wrong. Finally, I call the class back together, and each pair shares the most surprising fact they learned. For homework, the students write about their reactions to the activity. This has proved to be a rather effective way to help a class look behind the masks, and it can initiate useful conversations about prejudices and stereotyping.

Your Name _____

Period _____

Your Assumptions about _____

Locate the person whose name is written above. Write your assumptions about this person without talking to him/her.

   1. Favorite foods

   2. Favorite type of movie

   3. Favorite type of music

   4. Interests/hobbies

5. How many brothers/sisters?

6. Career plans

7. Favorite professional sport

8. Favorite subject in school

9. Favorite pet (include a likely name for the pet)

10. How long does it take this person to get ready in the morning?

Writing Prompts for the Assumptions Activity

General

Write about the experience of trading assumptions with a person you did not know very well.

Specific

- What was your response to the assumptions made about you?
- How accurate were you with your assumptions about your partner?
- Write about a situation where your assumptions got you into trouble.
- Write about a situation where your assumptions kept you out of trouble.
- Have you ever been "reduced to a stereotype"? Write about that situation.

CHAPTER 4

The Royalty

"Glory days well they'll pass you by"

—FROM THE BRUCE SPRINGSTEEN
COMPOSITION ENTITLED "GLORY DAYS"

E arly in my teaching career, I accepted a job at a junior high school in Monterey, California. At every age, kids are aware of the social hierarchy among their peers, but nowhere is it more clearly defined than in middle school. I was assigned a class that required me to teach geography for the first semester and sex education for the second semester. I had never taught either subject, but I was intrigued by the combination; in fact, I couldn't wait to see how in the world I'd pull off the segue from one unit of study to the next at midyear.

Becoming Aware of Your Own Prejudices

On the first day of school, I looked up to see Royalty enter the room. She was easy to spot, partly because she exuded a confidence far beyond her years and partly because when she sweetly asked a boy to switch seats with her so she could sit next to her boyfriend, he did so without the slightest protest. Julie and her boyfriend, Danny, would be chosen "cutest couple" on any school's superlatives list. They were adorable—attractive, socially adept, academically competent, and dressed always in the latest fashions. A few Rebels might make crude comments when Julie and Danny walked by, but the couple knew it was because those poor outcasts were just jealous. As was everyone else.

Fortunately for me, Julie and Danny gave me their seal of approval as a new teacher in the school, which reduced my discipline problems significantly. I appreciated their support but made sure that I did not treat them differently from anyone else in the class. As part of the sex education curriculum, the students were required to keep a journal of their "feelings" as we discussed the physical and emotional changes they were experiencing as they matured into adolescence. In reading these journals, I wasn't surprised to discover that many of the students in the class considered Danny's and Julie's lives to be perfect. What did surprise me was what Julie wrote in her journal. This object of so much envy was actually riddled with insecurities and self-loathing. Julie was intelligent enough to recognize that many of her family's problems were due to the constant strain of keeping up appearances. She was convinced that if any of her peers peeked underneath her carefully constructed facade, they would be repelled by what they saw.

I knew from the beginning that the sex education course would deal briefly with the physical changes the students were experiencing and focus far more extensively on the emotional roller coaster most of the students found themselves riding. Being careful to protect the identity of the writers, I created lessons exploring the struggles the students described in their journals. One discussion centered on living up to the expectations of others, and possibly because a few students had openly shared their fears and frustrations, Julie started describing to the class what it was like to be her. She began tentatively, but soon, she couldn't stop.

She told the class that she was painfully aware that the part of her most valued by others—her looks—was the source of her greatest insecurities. She watched as her mother lamented "losing her looks" and searched obsessively for the beauty products that would hold back time. Her mother often told Julie she was "lucky" to be born pretty, and Julie told the class that it was hard to feel any sense of accomplishment over an accident of birth. She also shared with us that she was exhausted at 13 from having to try so hard to cover up imperfections in herself and in her family. In fact, she alluded to some problems with alcoholism and verbal abuse in her home. Her classmates were stunned. They were silent for a while but then several thanked her for being brave enough to tell the truth. To his credit, Danny moved close and put his arm around her shoulders.

I'm not sure this discussion was a life-changing event for any of the students in the room, but they did have the opportunity to learn that most of us struggle with the same issues and often hide behind masks to protect ourselves. For me as a teacher, Julie was a reminder that I had to be careful to leave my personal prejudices, based on my own experiences as an adolescent, outside of my classroom. There were Julies in my junior high school when I was a kid, and I missed no opportunity to mock them whenever they crossed into my line of fire. In my mind, they needed an occasional fall from their high horses, and I was more than willing to oblige. I have known teachers who delight in embarrassing the "beautiful people" in their classes. When I listen to their glee over a particularly cutting remark they made in class to put a student like Julie in her place, I often suspect that subconsciously they've returned to the scene of their own humiliations to settle on old debt.

Documenting Your Grading System

In truth, it's a huge mistake to alienate these kids because they are powerful—they're the social leaders in any school and are capable of turning a class against the teacher at the turn of a cold shoulder. Sometimes, these students are the Jocks, the star athletes, and many of them are aware that an administrator who is a fan of a winning football team will go easy on the disruptive quarterback in your room. That doesn't mean that you let these students take over your class; this is why it is so important to have clearly outlined rules, consequences, and a grading system that are explained fully and enforced fairly (a sample grading policy is included at the end of this chapter).

Several times in my teaching career, I have been faced with a star athlete who was not used to having to worry about his grades because most teachers were afraid to tamper with his eligibility to play on the varsity teams. Robbie, a junior in my English class when I taught in Tennessee, excelled in every sport—football, basketball, baseball, track—he was the king of the Jocks. He wasn't necessarily a behavior problem in class; he would make a joke if he didn't know an answer, and his classmates were quick to cover for him. He just didn't take his work very seriously because he had already been courted by several colleges that guaranteed him a free ride if he would play for their schools. I had warned Robbie and his parents several times that he was failing my class, but no one took the threat seriously. When the first report cards were issued, Robbie was stunned to see an F as his quarter grade.

The next day, I was summoned to the principal's office, where Robbie, his parents, and the football coach were waiting for me. The meeting started out in a friendly manner, with the parents admitting that Robbie had never been good at English; then the principal jokingly said, "Oh, Ms. Gill doesn't know that much about sports—I'll bet you don't realize that an F in English would mean that Robbie couldn't start in next week's football game—you wouldn't do that to the boy, would you?" I assured the principal that I hadn't done that to the boy, he'd earned the 53% grade fair and square. The meeting started to go downhill from there, but luckily, I had brought Robbie's portfolio with me—this folder contained a complete record of Robbie's in-class writing and homework from the previous nine weeks. It also included a telephone log of the contacts with his parents, as well as a list of missed appointments that I had arranged so that Robbie could catch up on his work.

The parents silently leafed through the portfolio, but the coach got down to business, "Look, Vickie, why don't you just move his grade up to a passing score, and I will personally see to it that Robbie does better next quarter." I told the coach that I would never insult Robbie like that. They were all staring at me now. "If I put fake grades down for Robbie, what I'm saying to him is that he can't do it, that I don't think he's capable of earning a passing grade in English, and I don't think that's true." Robbie looked up at me, and I spoke directly to him. "You are a gifted athlete, no doubt, but you are also an intelligent young man, and you can learn to express yourself clearly in writing. I'm willing to show you what I know about improving your reading and writing skills if you are willing to accept the challenge."

I was going to toss in a clever sports analogy about him not needing a pinch hitter, but this was football season, and I didn't know what I was talking about anyway. I settled for smiling at the coach and saying, "From what the kids tell me, you would never encourage one of your athletes to take the easy way out." He told me I was right. The principal wasn't too happy, but luckily, I had worked to build a good relationship with Robbie and his parents long before this crisis developed, and we arranged some regular meeting times when Robbie and I could work one-on-one. He sat out one football game (luckily it wasn't homecoming), and the principal tweaked the rules so that Robbie needed only a D- to get back in the action. Some of the staff and students gave me a hard time about standing firm, but Robbie thanked me at the end of the year.

Again, I had to be careful that I was treating Robbie in exactly the same way I would treat any student—it would have taken a great deal of fudging to raise his 53% to passing when the report cards were issued. However, I remember a similar situation that occurred in the same high school several years later when a star basketball player earned a 59.89% in his senior English class—his teacher adamantly refused to round up the grade so that he could graduate, which I would have done. Mathematically it made sense, but this particular teacher relished her reputation as the "toughest grader on campus." In listening to her describe the conflict, I realized that she took a great deal of pleasure in the controversy it raised. She was a self-described nerd in high school who resented all of the attention lavished on the jocks, and I couldn't help but wonder if this was some kind of delayed revenge.

Treating Every Student Equally

Every high school has rich kids—the ones who pull into the school parking lot in brand new Mercedes or Porsches, waving at the teachers in their used Volvos or Fords. It would be wrong for me to bad-mouth their good fortune as they show off their latest vehicle, but sometimes, I can't resist asking in mock innocence, "My goodness, that's a beautiful car—where do you work?"

I have known clichéd "poor little rich kids" who, despite having every advantage laid at their feet, end up costing their families hundreds of thousands of dollars as they move in and out of one rehab after another. It broke my heart to hear a few years ago that the boy who was the envy of every guy and the fantasy of every girl in high school killed himself five years after graduating because his life became just too ordinary. I have also taught the son of one of the most famous men in the world, and he is universally respected because he is a hard-working, average student with zero sense of entitlement. It is foolish to stereotype these kids—teenagers are teenagers, and our job is to inspire them to live their lives in such a way that what they do for a living will improve the lives of others as well as their own.

I believe in equality in the classroom. The Royalty should not be given preferential treatment, but neither should it be assumed that they are snobs or unworthy. We teachers have to find ways to get to know our students as individuals who share common traits and desires with other human beings. You can earn respect for yourself as a teacher by setting up rules that are designed to create an atmosphere in the classroom where all students have the same opportunity to learn and by setting up consequences and a grading system that are administered fairly, regardless of a student's status in the social hierarchy. You will influence students who have been raised to expect preferential treatment far more effectively by resisting the urge to either cater to them or, on the other end of the spectrum, knock them down a few pegs. By treating all students with equality, yet recognizing their individuality, you can help each student develop and appreciate his or her own authentic sense of self-worth.

❧ **Classroom Management Tips** ❧

- Distribute clearly outlined rules, consequences, and grading policies that are explained fully and enforced fairly.
- Keep a portfolio with samples of each student's work. This file can be used for writing conferences to help students trace their progress. It can also be used to illustrate to the parents or administrators why a student is earning a poor grade in the class.
- Keep a file for each student that includes notes on parent contacts (dates, topic, suggestions). Include a copy of any information sent to administrators, counselors, or parents about concerns or achievements.
- Figure out a way to get to know each student as an individual—this could include journals or informal discussions outside of the classroom.
- Be careful that your personal prejudices are not influencing how you treat a student in the classroom. No one is prejudice-free; if you find yourself disliking a student based on past experiences, talk to a trusted colleague—it will help you to keep things in perspective.
- Create an environment that encourages positive risk-taking in your classroom.
- At the beginning of the year, distribute a Course Description that clearly explains your grading policy (see example on the next page).

༄ **Ms. Gill** ༄

English 9

Course Description:

This course is designed to improve each student's reading, writing, and thinking skills. Working independently, in small groups, and one-on-one with the instructor, the students will build individual portfolios containing a wide variety of writing samples. The purpose of the portfolio is to allow the student to clearly trace and demonstrate personal growth in the writing process. We will spend a great deal of time focusing on how to learn; therefore, the reading and writing techniques we practice in English 9 will prove useful in other academic classes, as well as in "the real world." Special attention will be paid to the improvement of each student's basic spelling, grammar, vocabulary, and study skills.

Grade Composition for Each Semester:

Tests & Formal Papers—45% (Final Exam is 10% of that total)
Quizzes—20%
Homework—25%
Effort Grade—10%

Effort Grade:

Each day students will receive a plus, a check, or a minus based on their preparedness for class and involvement in class activities. These marks translate into an effort grade, which is averaged in with the homework grade.

Excellent: All homework assignments completed, and student is fully involved in class activities.

Good: 80% of homework assignments completed, and/or student is often involved in class activities.

Satisfactory: 70% of homework assignments completed, and/or student is sometimes involved in class activities.

Poor: 60% of homework assignments completed, and/or student is rarely involved in class activities.

Unacceptable: 50% or less of homework assignments completed, and/or student's inappropriate behavior often disrupts class activities.

Materials for Class:

*_____ three-hole binder with dividers and extra notebook paper

*_____ black or blue ink pen

*_____ vocabulary book (I will give you this)

_____ highlighter for annotating text & "Post-it" tabs

*must be in class every day

CHAPTER 5

The Manipulators

Let's you and him fight.

—ERIC BERNE

If I had to pick one group of students who are the most difficult for me to handle in the classroom, it would have to be Manipulators. These kids are all about power and control, and they can be more disruptive to a class than a Rebel because they can cause long-term damage to the atmosphere in your classroom and your relationship with your students. The Rebels, Misfits, and Royalty are easy to spot; Manipulators can take you by surprise. And just to keep things interesting, Manipulators can cross over into any of the other categories of students; I have known Rebels, Victims, and Perfectionists who were also world-class Manipulators.

Recognizing the Games Students Play

Ms. Reese taught around the corner from my classroom in California. She was a first-year teacher, fresh out of college, full of idealism and enthusiasm.

I was a little concerned when I asked her if she needed any help in figuring out the rules for her classroom. She smiled sweetly and said that she didn't have a formal list of rules but would remind the students to be respectful in class. She added that she'd deal with specific problems as they came up—she liked to keep things positive. Ms. Reese was assigned to teach remedial math to the ninth graders, and she was excited to share with me the various activities that she had developed in her college courses to help her students master the basics and still have fun. I wanted to hug her; I probably did. I also told her to feel free to ask for help if she ever needed it. Remedial classes are never easy to teach and are often assigned to beginning teachers in what strikes me as some kind of perverse initiation rite.

Michael was what Ken Ernst described as an Uproar Player in his influential book on classroom management, *Games Students Play*. Michael wasn't particularly rude during his first class with Ms. Reese, but after a week, she learned to walk big circles around him. I believe their first tug-of-war was over homework. This is how the game is typically played: Ms. Reese has the students hand her their homework assignments as they exit her room at the end of class. The next day, she moves around the room handing back the graded papers, complimenting those who did a particularly good job and encouraging those who struggled with the assignment to meet her after school for some extra help. When she returns to the front of the class to begin the day's lesson, Michael calls out, "Hey, where's my homework? You forgot to hand it back to me." Ms. Reese smiles kindly:

Ms. Reese: Michael, you didn't hand anything to me when you left class yesterday—I remember.

Michael: Well, I remember that I did. Maybe you should check on your desk.

Ms. Reese: Michael, it's not on my desk. Last night when I recorded the grades in my grade book, you were the only person who didn't turn in an assignment.

Michael: You mean mine was the only assignment you lost!

Ms. Reese: No, you never gave it to me in the first place, but you can make it up tonight and give it to me tomorrow for reduced credit.

Michael: Why should my grade go down when you're the one who lost my homework!!??

This, of course, is accompanied by a sweeping, wide-eyed look of wonder at the unfairness of it all. Then, he makes his second move.

Michael: James, you remember me giving Ms. Reese my homework, don't you? I put it in the stack right before yours.

James: Yeah, man, I saw you—we left class at the same time.

Now there's a general stir in the classroom as those who hate Michael mutter, "Shut up, you know you didn't do it" and those who hang with Michael tell the others to shut up themselves and stay out of it. Ms. Reese is horribly aware that she's losing control of her class, and there's 40 minutes left in the period. "OK, OK, settle down. Michael, I'm going to believe you this time; I suppose your paper could have been lost in the shuffle. I'll give you credit just this once." Michael gives her a self-righteous "Thank you" and settles back into his seat. He allows her to begin teaching her lesson for the day.

Michael will pull the same stunt over and over in Ms. Reese's class, being careful to space out the "lost homework" accusations. There are plenty of other skirmishes he can win: tardies, sloppy penmanship on a test ("that's a 5, not a 3—anyone can see that!"). It won't be long before he has Ms. Reese well-trained; even when she catches him clearly in the wrong, she'll pretend she didn't notice so as to avoid the inevitable confrontation. It's just not worth it to her, it takes too much time, and she has 31 other students to think about. The problem is that she'll have five or six of Michael's protégées to deal with before the end of the first quarter ("You didn't give Michael a demerit when he was late!").

Ms. Reese asked for help after only two weeks. Luckily, Michael was a student in my freshman English class, so I knew all about him. He didn't give me quite the hard time he gave to Ms. Reese because he recognized that I was an experienced teacher, but it didn't take long for our first confrontation. I knew he was a Manipulator from the first day. I asked the students to take out a piece of paper and a pen to take a few notes, and he started to kick up dust over the fact that he didn't have a pen. I did. I always keep a big supply of pens and pencils in a jar at the front of the room—that is not a battle I choose to fight. The second I heard him start to create a scene over his lack of a writing utensil, I was at his side, pen in hand, and I sweetly and silently placed it on his desk. I had already started to give instructions to the class and never missed a beat. If I was in the mood to play a round of "Who Has the Power Now?" I could have followed Michael's lead and started "The Dance."

It goes like this: You begin your lesson; the Manipulator causes a minor distraction; you ask him to stop; he denies ever starting a problem—you started the problem; you tell him to speak respectfully; he shoots back, "Then why don't you?" Side step, side step, and twirl. The other students, depending on their motivations, either sink into their seats and wait for another classroom brushfire to die down or sit up and join in, backing their friend by confirming your shortcomings as a rather incompetent teacher of innocent youth, "He just needed a pen!" If it gets to this point, you'll trip over your own feet long before he does.

Easing from Teacher Control to Self-Control

Manipulators thrive on confrontation, and they especially enjoy a class where the teacher does not understand the nature of true power. We teachers can control our students with false power: threats, failing grades, isolation, public humiliation, trips to the office. These are temporary solutions at best. True power is when the students behave in our classes because they want what we have to offer, and they're willing to concede the control of the class to us so that they can get it. When I work with new teachers, the first concept I try to get them to accept is that we work for the students and their parents; they are our employers. We were hired because we are knowledgeable, but also because we see the worthiness in what we teach. A teacher who can demonstrate a love for her subject and who has the ability to prove to the students that proficiency in this discipline will help them achieve their personal goals—well, that's true power. The classroom management paradigm shifts from teacher control to self-control. You're selling, they're buying.

Recording Patterns of Behavior

When I sat down to help Ms. Reese with her tribulations with Michael, I tried to get her to focus on Michael's strengths. We both agreed that he was intelligent and clever and had a reasonably good sense of humor—visualizing him as an evil being gives him way too much power. I encouraged Ms. Reese to contact Michael's parents as soon as possible to open the lines of communication long before a real crisis emerged. I also suggested that Michael had most likely honed his manipulative skills at home, well before he entered school, so talking with the parents could be very illuminating.

Then we set up a system of documentation that would eliminate the majority of the "you did, I did" arguments Michael enjoyed. Ms. Reese brought in a special basket for homework that she placed on her desk. Without looking at Michael, Ms. Reese told the class that she was concerned about the occasional "lost" homework assignment, so from now on, all homework would be placed in the basket, and Ms. Reese would take a moment to quickly check off each student's name as the homework was turned in.

That was just the beginning. A seasoned pro like Michael could figure out a kink in the "basket of homework" system, so I helped Ms. Reese set up a file for him (and all of her students) so she could record the dates and the nature of various confrontations with Michael. Whenever Michael was late to class or accused Ms. Reese of losing his work or any other injustice, Ms. Reese gave him a slip of paper, asked him to describe the problem in a sentence or two, then sign and date it. She kept those in the file, too. When it came time for the inevitable parent-teacher conference about why this teacher was picking on this poor boy, Ms. Reese was able to spread the contents of the folder out on the table and show the parents the revealing pattern, carefully documented in Michael's own handwriting. Finally, I coached Ms. Reese to avoid any kind of accusation directed at Michael (sit out "the dance"), but to instead agree that a problem existed and to elicit the parents' and Michael's help in solving the problem. Together, the four of them devised a strategy to make sure that Michael's homework was placed in the basket every day; then after it was graded, Michael was responsible for putting the homework in a file that stayed in Ms. Reese's classroom for safekeeping. The entire tone of the conversation was focused on devising solutions, rather than assigning blame. Because Ms. Reese was a new teacher, it was important that she had an experienced teacher in the room when she held this conference. Ms. Reese asked her department chair to attend, which is how I heard about how well this played out. He was a huge help because, having dealt with a number of Manipulators in his time, he added a well-placed chuckle when Ms. Reese dumped out the slips of paper on which Michael himself had admitted to problem after problem after problem.

Picking and Choosing Your Battles

It's hard for a beginning teacher to anticipate all of the petty annoyances that can lead to a full-scale battle for power in the classroom. At the beginning of the year, Ms. Reese told the class to be on time but would turn a blind eye to the occasional tardy student. This, of course, blossomed into an epidemic, and soon, more students were late to her class than on time. And there were always the brave few who pushed the boundaries and breezed in 5 or 10 minutes late to a 50-minute class. Ms. Reese needed a system with clear, simple consequences that she could sell as "fair" to the students. Here's what she did: She waited for a day when everyone was on time (so no one felt "picked on"), then told the class that she was concerned about the number of students coming in late. She pointed out that she started class on time every day because they had so much to do, and she didn't want anyone to miss out on any of this great information that would help them achieve their goals (she'd spent some time selling them on the usefulness of math). So, she was instituting a new policy for tardies, starting today. A general groan went up from the class, but Ms. Reese plowed ahead.

Now I know that stuff happens, any one of us can be held up on our way to class—why, occasionally someone will stop to ask me a question in the office, and I'll be a few minutes late myself. So here's what we'll do: Right now, I'm giving each one of you two free passes to be late to class—no questions asked. If someone bumps into you in the hallway and your books fly everywhere, or the bathrooms are crowded, or the counselor keeps you in her office too long—no problem! Just enter the class quietly, sit down, and get to work. I don't want you to interrupt the lesson to give me your excuse; it doesn't matter—you have two free tardies each semester. After class, I'll mark the tardy in my roll book, but there will be no consequence.

On the third tardy, do the same thing—come in quietly, don't offer an excuse or disturb the class—and I'll make a note to turn in a demerit for you. You'll get a demerit for every tardy thereafter—and in our school, you have detention after the fourth demerit, so I know this won't become a problem. If for some bizarre reason, you are 10 or more minutes late to class, go to the principal's office first because that is the same as skipping class.

Ms. Reese gleefully told me later that the kids just stared at her—they couldn't really protest because she was giving them a gift, but at the same time, they knew that they would now be held accountable for coming to class on time.

Ms. Reese's first year had its ups and downs, but she learned a great deal about the need for specific rules and specific consequences so that the students would all feel they were being treated fairly and so a student like Michael couldn't accuse her of delivering a consequence just because she didn't like him.

⤳ Falling Into the Guilt Trap ⤳

One of the most frustrating interactions you can have with a Manipulator is what I would call an "irresolvable disagreement." The student is angry about an action you took or a decision you made and wants to make you feel terrible because the consequences were severe. A perfect example is when a teacher catches a student smoking on campus. Few teachers are horrified by a kid sneaking a cigarette—we may have done the same thing ourselves. So when they smell cigarette smoke coming out of a restroom, many teachers will bang on the door, tell whoever's in there to come out, roll their eyes when the kid swears that the stalls had been full of smoke when he went in there, and send the student on his way with a warning. In many schools, the consequence for smoking on campus is a week's suspension, so some teachers look the other way because they don't want to be the one who caused the kid such a severe punishment. You and I know that the consequence was the result of a choice the kid made, but Manipulators in particular are very good at redirecting the guilt right back to the teacher.

One morning last May, I was walking between classes through the school parking lot to get something from my car when I noticed a freshman girl and a senior boy sitting in another car talking. In my school, it's against the rules for students to be in the parking lot without a pass during the school day, and the girl, Regina, had been the source of some concern among the faculty because her attitude in general had become very negative as she tried to fit in with a group of much older students.

I knocked on the glass, smiled, and motioned for them to open the window. They looked embarrassed and immediately got out of the car, and

Regina said defensively, "We were just talking." I told her I was sure that was true, but they knew they were breaking the rules by choosing Robert's car as the place to talk, and I needed to let the principal know where they were. Robert admitted he was in the wrong place at the wrong time, but Regina was furious with me for making a big deal out of such an innocent situation. I told her that I would have done the same thing with any student I found in the parking lot and repeated that one of my jobs as a teacher was to make sure she was safe. She insisted she was safe—"We weren't doing anything! We were just talking!" I told her I believed her, but that the school had made the rules about the parking lot because all sorts of problems had occurred there in the past.

The principal called Robert's and Regina's parents, and she wouldn't speak to me for the remainder of the year. When school resumed in September, Regina was cool at first, but she had signed up to work on the school's literary journal and I was the adviser, so we slowly began to rebuild our relationship. In fact, by October, we seemed to be getting along just fine. Then one day, Regina stayed after class to help me put away some materials because we both had the next period free. I thanked her and added that I was glad we'd become friends again. She plunked herself down in a chair and said, "But I'm still mad at you for ruining everything when you told on me and Robert."

I was a little startled that she was still stewing about an incident that happened more than five months earlier, but I dutifully sat down opposite her and explained that on that morning in May, I really couldn't just pretend that I didn't see her in the car. She said that I could have just given them a warning and that I didn't have to turn it into such a big deal. She added that because of the mess I had caused, she was not able to go to the prom with Robert, and now he'd gone away to college, things would never be the same, and it was all my fault. As I sat there and listened to this harangue, I felt like laughing because her anger seemed so random and illogical, but I tried to be patient and once again clarify that it was my responsibility as her teacher to watch out for her—at the time she was 14 and Robert was 18.

Rather than calm her down, the more I tried to explain myself, the more angry she became. This went on for way longer than it should have—I was hoping to clear up any misunderstandings and get us back to where our relationship had been just an hour before, but Regina was having none of it. I finally got up and told her I needed to get ready for my next class and that our discussion was going nowhere. She grabbed my arm and said, "But you ruined everything!" I turned back to her in frustration and asked, "What would you like me to do, create some kind of time machine so we can go back to last May and do everything differently?" She shot back: "Yes, that's what I want." I just stared at her for a few seconds and told her that the whole discussion had passed bizarre a half hour ago, and I needed to go. She followed me for a bit, but I didn't stop.

That evening, I couldn't get the ridiculous argument out of my mind. I kept second-guessing how I should have handled it, and I did feel kind of sorry that she missed going to prom, even though in my mind she was too young to date an 18-year-old, and besides, I wasn't the one who had made that decision. The next morning, I woke up with an idea that I knew could either help or bomb horribly. I sat at the computer and typed five simple sentences in which I summarized what I heard her say to me the previous day. I printed it out, put it in an envelope, and wrote her name on the outside. When she passed by my classroom in the morning, I asked if I could talk with her for just a couple of minutes. She looked a little annoyed but didn't walk away. I shared with her my concerns about our discussion— not the "I'm right, you're wrong" debate—but the fact that it looped around endlessly on itself with no clear solution in sight. I said, "You know that there is no way to go back in time, but we can take a huge step forward today," and I handed her the paper.

I went on, "Sometimes in an argument, it isn't so much about demanding that the problem be fixed right now—what you really want is a sense that you've been heard. So, I wrote down what I heard you say. Read it and tell me if I understood your point of view correctly." She laughed and looked at me like I was crazy, but she started reading. I wrote the note in her voice, trying to use her own words as often as I could, "You walked through the parking lot and saw Robert and me sitting in the car and told us to get out, but we weren't doing anything. . . ."

She read it twice, then said that one sentence was wrong—it wasn't that her parents wouldn't let her go to the prom. Robert didn't ask because everything got so weird between them after they got in trouble. I told her to circle that and anything else she read that wasn't correct. Then I said, "As I wrote, I tried to see this from your point of view. Some time today, I want you to write down what I said—just a few sentences that sum up how I perceived the situation." Regina threw the paper on the table and said, "I can't do that!" And I said, "I know, it's hard, but if you could ever learn to try to look at an argument from the other person's point of view, that would be a tremendous advantage for you. It's not that you have to agree, it's just that you are able to state accurately what the other person was trying to say."

Regina glared at me and walked out the door, then turned around and said, "Give me the paper—I have to look at how you wrote it if I'm going to write back." It took her a couple of days, but with a little prodding, she finally handed me her version of my version. I had to correct a few things, and we agreed to cross out a bit of editorializing on her part, but three sentences remained in which she accurately rephrased what I had been trying to say in the heat of the argument—it started out, "I saw Robert and you sitting in his car, and it's against the rules for students to be in the parking lot. . . ."

Manipulators can be very good at spotting the weaknesses in others and using those soft spots to get what they want. In the story at the beginning of this chapter, Michael knew that Ms. Reese wanted to be recognized and accepted as a fair teacher, so he shouted "Unfair!" at every opportunity, which sure enough caused her to back down at first. I'm used to getting along with most of my students and feeling trusted by them, so Regina knew it would drive me crazy if she made me think that a poor decision on my part had caused her a great deal of pain. When she started the argument that day, I verbally parried back and forth with her for 45 minutes. My common sense told me to keep it short and get out, but I allowed myself to be manipulated into participating in a disagreement that had no resolution. Later on, I found out that Robert was coming home from college soon, and I believe Regina wanted me to admit that I'd made a mistake and try to make amends by talking her parents into letting her go out with him. The fact that she was able to get a rise out of me was proof enough that I felt badly about turning her in to the principal in the first place, and I fell right into Regina's guilt trap.

Protecting Yourself by Staying Professional

Most of these dramas are kids' stuff, but some Manipulators take it to extremes. I knew one bright, talented young teacher who lost his job because he had a conference with a girl in his classroom with the door closed. The girl, who was a classic Manipulator, accused him of making sexual advances toward her, and it came down to his word against hers. I learned later that she had a crush on him, and this was revenge because he did not respond to her advances.

I've been the victim of this type of manipulation myself: I was sitting in the sun at lunch correcting papers when a girl in my second-period class, April, plopped down next to me. We started chatting about this and that and ended up laughing over something particularly annoying that a boy had done in my class that morning. Ben swore he had completed an essay that was due that day but claimed that his computer had freaked out and the file had been erased. I doubt there is a teacher in the world who has not heard the "dog/computer ate my homework" excuse way too many times, and I gave the boy my standard response, "If you'll look at the instructions I handed out, I advised you to make several backup copies of your work for just such a crisis. I guess you'll have to rewrite your essay and turn it in tomorrow. As you know, I reduce the grade by five points for every day it's late." Ben was stunned by the unfairness of it all, but I quickly moved the class on to the next activity.

April and I laughed about Ben's flirty attempt at the end of class to get me to just give him credit for the essay anyway, and I casually said, "Yeah, old Ben and his missing work. You'd think he'd feed the computer once in awhile, since it eats his homework on a regular basis—other teachers tell me he's used that as an excuse in their classes, too." We went on to talk about a number of trivial matters, such as whether or not it would rain later in the week, the fantastic new ice cream shop that opened two blocks from the school, our current favorite songs. When I went home that day, I forgot about the entire conversation.

The next morning, Ben stormed into my classroom and accused me of calling him a liar behind his back. For a minute, I had no idea what he was talking about, but then he mentioned April had called him to let him know that I had told her that most of his teachers thought he was lying when he said he was having problems with his computer. Technically, he was right, and I apologized. I told him I didn't say he was a liar, but he did seem to have more than his share of trouble with getting his work turned in on time. I calmed him down as much as I could; then we discussed several ways of making backup copies of his work. He and I already had established a friendly relationship, and that alone probably saved me from an awkward meeting with his parents in my principal's office. I also made a point of sitting down to talk privately with April. I told her what I told Ben and added that I was surprised that she felt our conversation was serious enough to merit a phone call to him. I knew better than to alienate her, but I also knew to keep any future exchanges on as professional a level as possible. The boundary between getting to know your students on a friendly basis and maintaining your professional distance is something that all teachers must learn to recognize.

Over the past 28 years, I have dealt with students who caused problems because they were too inexperienced to fully understand the likely outcome of their actions. I have also worked with pathological liars who were incapable of telling the difference between reality and their version of the truth. Despite the heartache these kids can cause, I do not think any of them are "bad"—they're just operating on the system they've devised to survive their childhood. If you think about it, we're all Manipulators on one level or another. In the classroom, I consider myself a benevolent Manipulator, because I am using all sorts of techniques that will allow me to influence my students' motivations and behaviors. One of our jobs as teachers is to help the malevolent Manipulators we find in our classrooms learn to use their formidable powers for good. As always, it all comes down to getting to know our students as individuals so that we can teach them to believe that true power is more satisfying and longer lasting than the false power they've been wielding.

✌ **Classroom Management Tips** ✌

- Make sure you are not modeling false power to the students as you handle problems in the classroom.
- Create a method to document confrontations so that a pattern of negative behaviors can be traced and solutions can be devised. Do not rely on your memory or your word carrying more weight than their word.
- Focus on solutions, not blame. The point isn't to force the student to say "you're right"—you probably are. The point is to solve the problem.
- Spend some time selling your product—demonstrate to the students the usefulness of the skills you are teaching.
- Shift the paradigm of the class from teacher control to self-control as soon as possible and compliment the class as a whole when they've had a productive day. Thank them for their help.
- When disciplining even the most difficult students, acknowledge what they're doing right before you focus on what they're doing wrong. Along this line, get to know the students well enough so that you can describe their positive traits—ask other teachers, coaches, and administrators if nothing comes to mind.
- Not all parents or guardians have access to e-mail, but on the second day of school, I ask my students to have their parents send a short "Hi There" e-mail to my account so that I have the parent/guardian e-mail address in my computer. This has become an easy way for me to send a quick note home.
- Keep parents up-to-date on students' progress or lack of progress—no surprises. Document your parent contacts (see example on next page).

❧ Parent/Guardian Contact Log ❧

E-mail—Telephone—Letter—Conference
(circle one)

Date _____

Student's Name _____

Parent/Guardian's Name _____

Notes: _____

_____

_____

_____

_____

_____

❧ Parent/Guardian Contact Log ❧

E-mail—Telephone—Letter—Conference
(circle one)

Date _____

Student's Name _____

Parent/Guardian's Name _____

Notes: _____

_____

_____

_____

_____

_____

CHAPTER **6**

The Victims

"Everybody's got a hungry heart"

—FROM THE BRUCE SPRINGSTEEN
COMPOSITION ENTITLED "HUNGRY HEART"

Victims are important players in any high school drama because they offer the more aggressive students a chance to test their powers. Victims are often unwilling participants—for example, the smallest boy in the ninth grade—and may struggle against disadvantages that they cannot control. Others, however, actually invite the victimization because negative attention in their minds is better than no attention at all. The most familiar scenario is the weaker kid who is physically attacked by a bully. Most of us don't think of it this way, but there are two victims in that scene—the person being attacked and the attacker. We rarely think of bullies as victims, but their physical aggression is most likely a learned behavior and is often a weak cover for frustration and low self-esteem. I often think of a sad cartoon in which the father comes in from a bad day at work and smacks the older son, the older son pops the younger brother, the younger brother kicks the dog, and the dog snaps at the cat—victims all. I cannot imagine a teacher, whether a seasoned veteran or a tentative beginner, who would not immediately and decisively intervene to protect a student who was being physically threatened by another student. However, some types of victimization are far more subtle and difficult to address without exposing the Victim to further harassment.

Discerning False Power From True Power

It's likely that all of us have been victims and bullies in our lives. As with walking or learning to ride a bike, we have to make a few false steps in order to catch our balance. Toddlers are likely to bop another two-year-old on the head when he or she innocently grabs the crayon they were just about to use, and in turn, they'll receive a few well-placed bops themselves. Most children are guided by their parents or caregivers to find more peaceful and socially acceptable ways to get what they want; however, some carry the methods for gaining and losing power that they learned in the nursery well into their adult lives. I see this all of the time in my classroom. One of the first lessons I teach every year is the difference between False Power and True Power. This is easy to bring up in an English classroom because just about any work of fiction I choose has a plot in which someone wants something that another will not give up, and much of this has to do with power and control. I've taught in schools where hazing had become enough of a problem that specialists were invited to speak to the faculty.

It's difficult to deal with this type of behavior if you are not there to witness it. A few years ago, I had a student in my class who quickly gained a reputation for bullying some of the younger boys. He had been called into the principal's office on a number of occasions for his inappropriate behavior, but in fact, Zach rather enjoyed his image as someone to be feared. In the first few weeks of school, I went out of my way to develop a positive connection with Zach so he'd be open to learning something from me. After I heard several stories about his harassment of other students, I wrote *False Power* and *True Power* on the Board and asked the students to write in their journals for a few minutes about the difference between the two. Several students shared their ideas, but when it came to Zach, he said, "False power is where you can't get anyone to do what you say. True power is this." And he held up his fist. Instead of giving him the expected indignant authority-figure reaction, I just shook my head and offered him my most sympathetic expression, "Do you really believe that's true? How sad." Zach was startled, to say the least. I went on to tell him that I could see he was really mixed up about the whole power thing, but that I'd do everything I could to help him discover his true power. He thought I was nuts at first, but over the semester, I was able to help him understand two concepts: One, physically forcing someone to comply lasts only as long as the bully is present whereas changing someone's mind lasts forever; two, Zach himself was a victim—someone somewhere along the line had convinced him that no one would listen to him unless they were forced. How sad.

Protecting Victims From Themselves

We as teachers have the responsibility to protect our students from the Zachs of the world, but sometimes, victims can actually initiate the bullying themselves. Susan, a sophomore, had very few friends because of her alarming inability to read social cues. One afternoon, I found myself in a van with another teacher and seven students, including Susan, headed across town to participate in a community service project. The captain of the football team, Eric, and two of his buddies were passengers in the van, along with several younger students. I knew it would take about 30 minutes to reach our destination, so I blithely tried to engage the kids in conversation. I tossed out a few random questions in an attempt to get everyone talking, something like, "What are your plans for the next vacation?" or "What are you reading in your English class?" Susan immediately jumped in to answer the first question, and then proceeded to speed-rap her way through a random assortment of stories about her life. At first, the other students listened politely, but whenever they tried to interject a comment or a story of their own, Susan would cut them off with a rude remark and continue to dominate the conversation. I kept trying to open the conversation up to the rest of the students, but Susan continued to interrupt. At first, the other kids laughed and rolled their eyes at Susan's prickly comments, but the other teacher and I shifted uncomfortably in our seats as the atmosphere grew more hostile.

After Susan launched into another story of a game she and her brother had played as kids, Eric started asking Susan questions, feigning fascination. The other students snickered or outright laughed as he led Susan on—"So, you were a pirate, huh? Tell me about your outfit—did you have a sword strapped to your leg? I'll bet you liked that." I began giving Eric the evil eye, but he never indicated by his facial expression or tone of voice that he was anything other than enthralled by Susan's childhood tales. Nothing he said was rude on the surface, but everyone in the van could read the sarcasm in every remark he made. I could tell by the change in Susan's expression that she realized Eric was making fun of her, and I tried several times to bail her out of the conversation, but she couldn't or wouldn't stop. It was painful to watch. I could have called Eric on his nonsense there and then, but it wouldn't have improved the mood and could have caused serious harassment for Susan later on.

Finally in desperation, I blurted out that I had a very funny story about something that happened with my cat over the weekend—a story that anyone could tell I was making up on the spot—but even then Susan interrupted me to talk about *her* cat. The other teacher and I managed to keep things from getting out of hand, but we could not wait to get out of that van.

If this had occurred in my classroom, I never would have let it go that far. I can protect a Susan because I am in charge of the pace and focus of the lesson. I can allow Susan to have a voice, but a classroom discussion would rarely morph into a random social conversation such as we attempted to have. However, I could not let the kids think that what occurred that afternoon was acceptable. I found Eric the next day and discussed with him how inappropriate his actions were. He protested that he was just egging her on because she wouldn't let anyone else speak. I told him I understood, but I also said that I considered him to be one of the leaders of the school, and what he did was a cheap use of his power. I asked for his help if he ever noticed anyone else picking on Susan just because she was an easy mark. We parted on good terms.

Then I made a point of talking with Susan when we were alone and had a bit of time. I was honest about the discomfort I felt in the van and asked her to tell me how she perceived the situation. At first, she brushed off Eric's rude behavior as typical of most of the teenagers she knew, but after a bit, she admitted that she hated being laughed at like that. Slowly and gently, I got her to see that she had a way of inviting the ridicule because she often didn't notice the social cues that the rest of us rely on when we interact with other people. Susan and I worked out a signal where I would touch her arm if she was dominating a conversation, and several other teachers tried to help her to notice and support the give and take that is essential to any discussion, whether it takes place in an academic or social setting. She and I met off and on for the rest of the semester—I shared with her Eric Berne's theory of transactional analysis, which helped her intellectualize the innate social instincts she lacked. I also encouraged her to start writing her stories down and offered to read some of them. I had to walk a fine line with Susan—I was hired to be her teacher, not her savior.

✑ **Supporting Rather Than Enabling** ✑

We teachers love to help—we're really good at it and every one of us has had or will have the heady experience of a student letting us know "you've changed my life." That comment never fails to honor and frighten me at the same time. My heart goes out to kids who, for one reason or another, are at a loss as to how to develop healthy, close relationships with their peers. Victims often feel ostracized and lack friends who are willing to relieve their loneliness. It is tempting for a loving, empathetic teacher to attempt to fill that void, but in truth, that teacher is more likely to become an enabler rather than a friend.

This happened to a well-meaning colleague of mine. Ms. Perry had been teaching for three years when Mary was assigned to her homeroom group. Mary was a shy, attractive 14-year-old who didn't know anyone when she transferred to our school, and Ms. Perry went out of her way to be encouraging as Mary tried to acclimate to her new environment. After a couple of weeks, Mary was invited to join a popular group of girls for lunch and soon found herself in the middle of a tug-of-war between the two leaders of the group, Dani and Jessie. One of the girls stopped speaking to the other because they both liked the same boy. Dani snagged Mary first and told her all sorts of mean things Jessie had said behind their backs. Soon, Mary found herself the victim of rumors and insults based on the fact that she had sided with Dani. Mary confided in Ms. Perry, who wisely counseled her to stay out of the whole mess.

As predictable as the plot of a bad soap opera, Dani and Jessie patched up their friendship before the end of the month, and both denounced Mary as having caused much of the trouble. Now Mary was not welcomed at any table in the cafeteria, so Ms. Perry allowed her to eat in her classroom. She didn't want Mary to be alone at such a traumatic time, so Ms. Perry started eating in her room, too. As Mary talked about her failure to fit in at her new school, she also shared stories about family problems and other heartaches from the past. Ms. Perry was a sympathetic ear, and Mary poured out her heart to her. Knowing that Mary spent most of her weekends alone in her room reading, Ms. Perry offered to take Mary with her when she went shopping on Saturday. They had a wonderful time, and Ms. Perry was glad to spend a little extra time with such a sweet, sad girl.

Over the next few months, Mary became more and more dependent. Soon, Mary was calling her teacher at her home in the evenings. At first, Ms. Perry didn't mind the intrusion—she herself had been lonely as a child and would have loved to have a teacher who was willing to spend a little extra time with her. As the demands for her attention became greater and greater, however, Ms. Perry began to pull away. This created true desperation on Mary's part; she would become hysterical—anything to pull her confidante back in. Instead of providing support for a lonely child, Ms. Perry unwittingly helped to create a codependent relationship with Mary—one that was not likely to end satisfactorily for either person.

Right now, I have a close friend who is 15 years my junior, but as we get older, a large span in experience becomes less and less meaningful. That is not true for a teacher and a student in elementary or secondary school. We can become good friends with our students, but we are doing these kids a disservice if we allow our friendship to fill the space they should have open to create healthy bonds with their peers. Ms. Perry's and Mary's story did not end well. It was inevitable that Ms. Perry had to place some restrictions on how far Mary could intrude into her teacher's personal life. Mary viewed this as a betrayal; her wounds were not healed, and Mary thought of herself as even more of a victim than before. During that time, she made little progress in learning how to make friends with her classmates, but she also learned to shy away from adults as well as her peers.

Teaching is a heady profession. We teachers truly can change the lives of children. Kids like to spend time with us because we're sincerely interested in their well-being. But we have to be mindful of this awesome opportunity that we've been given to influence and guide people at the most impressionable time in their lives. Especially when dealing with children who have been victims in their families or in other social settings, we have to be careful that we're supporting students as they search for solutions to their own problems, rather than finding the answer for them, or even worse, trying to become the solution ourselves.

✎ **Classroom Management Tips** ✎

- If your school does not have a new teacher-mentoring program, find a supportive colleague to talk with on a regular basis. That person will help you decide when your relationship with a student is in danger of becoming codependent.
- I think it's wiser to give your students your e-mail address rather than your home phone number if you don't mind talking with them outside of school hours. That will allow you to think about your responses and keep the relationship on a professional level.
- If you do invite a student to your house socially, invite one or two other students as well to help the shy student begin to make friends in his or her own age group.
- Unless a victim is in physical danger, talk to the bully privately to help him or her save face and to protect the victim from reprisal.
- If you should encounter a threatening situation involving a bully and a victim, get an administrator involved as soon as possible.
- Try to think of ways to discuss the nature of power as part of your lessons in class. It's not difficult to do in English or history, but if you're aware that bullying is becoming a real problem at your school, you can actually take some class time to address your concerns with your students and give them a chance to discuss the issue. It may take a few minutes from your mandated curriculum, but this is one of those judgment calls that will be easy to defend as a responsible teacher who is concerned about the well-being of the students. A student who is afraid of verbal or physical abuse cannot concentrate on the regular classwork anyway.
- At the beginning of the school year, I spend some time helping my students generally define their future career goals. Often, in the ninth grade, 75% of the students will know exactly what they want to do, and the remaining 25% have no clue or only a vague idea. I get them to talk or write about the things they enjoy doing in their spare time, and sometimes, they just write down what type of work

they'd prefer to do if they had to (indoor/outdoor, paperwork/hands-on, group/alone, etc.). I find it helpful to shift their focus from doing the work in my class to earn a grade to doing the work in my class to strengthen the reading, writing, and people skills they'll need to be successful on the job. By the end of the first month, I give them an assignment called "Writing in the Real World" that is due after Thanksgiving break (see examples on the next two pages). Basically, the students are to find a person who is working in a career that interests him or her and ask for a sample of typical on-the-job writing that they will later share with the class. I do this partly because it motivates the students to put in the extra work necessary to improve their writing skills. I also give this assignment to help the Victims (and the others) to broaden their microfocus on their tiny universe and to try to visualize the opportunities that await them in the much larger "real world."

Name: _____

∽ **Writing in the Real World** ∽

Date Due: _____

- Locate someone who is working in a career in which you are interested. You may do this in person, on the telephone, through e-mail, or in the form of a well-written business letter.
- Ask this person for a sample of the type of writing he or she does on the job.
- Bring the writing sample to share with the class by the due date. (You may bring it to class before that date, if you choose.)
- In searching for someone working in your field of interest, ask for help from family members, friends, parents of friends, teachers, administrators, staff—literally anyone you run into.
- Career opportunities are all about networking. This is a great chance for you to contact someone who can tell you a great deal about your future goals. Be sure to ask the person about the training he or she needed to qualify for the job.

Name _____

Period _____

Your Assumptions About Your Chosen Career:

Before you contact someone working in the career you are interested in, make some assumptions about that job. When you ask for your on-the-job writing sample, ask these questions as well to find out how accurate your expectations are.

Job Title: _____

1. The on-the-job duties:

2. The benefits (think about both pay and job satisfaction):

3. The type of training required to qualify for this job:

4. The working conditions (environment):

5. The type of writing you'll be required to do on the job:

CHAPTER 7

The Extraordinary

I want to stay as close to the edge as I can without going over. Out on the edge you see all kinds of things you can't see from the center.

—KURT VONNEGUT, JR.

School systems are designed to teach "regular" kids and to accommodate for the Extraordinary. I don't like to think of any of my students as ordinary, but the majority can seem rather normal in contrast to the kids whose brains work differently or who have lived through experiences that the rest of us can barely imagine. As far as classroom management is concerned, I'm a firm believer that we teachers should develop a simple, logical system of rules and consequences that is implemented in such a way that students do not feel that the teacher has favorites or manages the classroom based on moods and temper. However, one of the reasons that teachers have not been replaced by computers or a series of well-produced lectures on DVD is that we are professionals who can make judgment calls when faced with unusual circumstances. We should be committed to helping our students access and use the ideas and skills that make up the disciplines we teach, but the thrill and the challenge of teaching is that we're working with human beings who do not all respond or operate in the same way. That's why teaching is rarely boring or routine—we meet new faces, new talents, new needs, new challenges every year, and in some schools, every hour.

✑ Helping to Calm a Noisy Mind ✑

When I taught in the Tennessee public school system, I created a vocational English class for seniors who were at risk for dropping out of school. Many had caused serious discipline problems in the regular classes, so I was free to design my own curriculum as long as I kept the kids relatively quiet and in school (loss of ADA money was a concern for the cash-strapped county). After a few years, I was able to talk the school board into purchasing 10 new computers to line the walls of my classroom. I worked in the back of the school in a large room that had been used to teach cosmetology, so it was outfitted with lots of plugs, and after three decades of teaching, it remains my favorite type of working space. Inspired by the system used in most elementary school classrooms, I divided my 30 students into three groups: 10 on computers practicing vocabulary, spelling, grammar, and writing skills; 10 at their seats working independently; and 10 in a small group working with me. We don't have a great deal of control over choosing our classrooms, but even in a small space, it's important to arrange the furniture so that there is some room for students to move around and for teachers to work with the kids as individually as possible.

One of my main goals is to develop a positive relationship with each of my students, and the best way to do that is to give them a sense that I know them as individuals rather than as anonymous members of a large group. I spend a great deal of time gathering information about the reading and writing levels of my students at the beginning of the school year so I can create a curriculum that will best serve their individual needs; but

I also need to know about any extraordinary circumstances that may prevent my students from focusing on their studies.

Jeremy entered my classroom with an abysmal GPA and the threat of a last chance. Instead of causing overt behavior problems for his teachers, Jeremy just sat and refused to do any work. He was difficult partly because he was so passive and uncommunicative—he just didn't care. He had been in therapy, but he was making little progress and had refused to take any of the medications prescribed to make him more responsive. His counselor had devised a special schedule for Jeremy that required him to be in school for only half of the day—he took my class and two vocational classes. He'd been removed from his math class because he walked out when his teacher demanded that Jeremy "drop the attitude" and become an active participant in class or else. The other students walked big circles around him—they knew his history, and Jeremy didn't seem interested in making friends. Jeremy missed the first two weeks of his senior year, so when he joined my class I asked him to sit at a table by himself and take some pretests to give me an idea as to how I could help him. I didn't react to his sullen stares or his listless manner—I find that there are times when I need to give my students the impression that I can read their minds and times when I need to play dumb. I believe part of the art of teaching is developing an instinct for what to pay attention to and what to ignore. I'm not sure what got him going, but Jeremy decided to show me what he could do on those pretests—possibly just to let me know that I had nothing to teach him. He flew through an SAT vocabulary pretest and wrote two pages on my generic prompt designed to give me an idea about the students' basic writing skills: "Imagine that it's 10 years in the future, and we run into each other. Where would you like to be and what would you like to have accomplished?" Jeremy had only one goal for the future—to be dead like his father, but this was written by a gifted young man who as a writer was fully alive. Our class met right before lunch, so on the second day, I asked Jeremy to stay for a few minutes to talk with me. In truth, I asked him to stay for a few minutes so I could carry on what I knew would be a one-sided conversation; I also knew I had one chance to get this right. I started out by describing the curriculum I had planned for most of my students, centering on increasing their vocabulary, fine-tuning their writing skills, and improving their reading comprehension. He stared at the floor. Then I shoved his vocabulary pretest in front of him and said, "You didn't miss a single word—I have nothing to teach you there." Then I took out his writing pretest and said, "And there's only one conclusion I can draw from this." He looked up, waiting to see if I'd react in shock, disgust, or sympathy. I just leaned back in my chair, smiled, and said, "You, my friend, have one noisy mind." He looked me fully in the eyes for the first time, and I went on. "Usually with my students, I'm trying to speed up the way they process information, but I'd love to try to help you turn the whole thing down a notch or two—what do you think?" He didn't answer but was listening, so I plunged ahead. "My guess is that you may have tried to self-medicate with drugs? alcohol?" He nodded very slightly, but I noticed it. "And in general, you're looking for something to just keep it at a hum. What kind of music do you like?" He looked a little startled by the question but named a few bands I'd never heard of—ah, he spoke. I told him that I taught journalism and that the students put out a biweekly newspaper. We needed a writer of his caliber to contribute opinion pieces and music reviews, and I asked him if he'd be willing to join the staff. He didn't respond, so I told him to think about it and let me know the next day. After our conversation, I immediately high-tailed it to the office and persuaded my principal to allow Jeremy to earn his English credit in my journalism class. The principal reluctantly agreed, partly because he didn't expect Jeremy to stay in school long enough for it to make a difference. But Jeremy did stay through to graduation; he never talked much in class but because of his extraordinary writing skills and unique perspective on the world, Jeremy's reviews and opinion pieces became one of the most popular features of the school newspaper.

Seeking Help From the Experts

It's not practical, in fact, I doubt it's possible for us to tailor lesson plans to meet each student's needs. Many teachers aim at the center and adjust for the students who learn at either end of the spectrum. Students under the special education umbrella enter your classes with individualized education plans (IEPs) that allow you to fall back on the advice and guidance of experts to design a curriculum and discipline plan that will help a mainstreamed student succeed in your classes. When I'm introducing my classroom rules and consequences, I have all students sign the rules contract saying that they have read and understood the rules. Whether students have been diagnosed with Down's syndrome or autism, I give them the opportunity to sign the same as their peers, but I know that I'll talk to that student's special ed teacher to create a modified plan for the student's behavior. It wasn't always that way, but nowadays all credentialed teachers are well-versed in the adjustments they will need to make, by law, for these students' special needs.

Dealing With Extraordinary Circumstances

My students will tell you that I teach by telling stories, and at my age, I have many stories to tell. Sometimes I'm trying to illustrate a point or create a connection between a work of fiction and real life. Sometimes as I tell a story, I look right into the eyes of a student who is struggling with the same demons and hold her gaze when I deliver the punch line. I want to let the student know I recognize who she is; I want the student to know that I view her as unique. Sometimes I tell stories that are designed to inspire—to help us get over ourselves. This is one I tell when I'm dealing with a student who is acting out over the petty frustrations of everyday life.

Jonathan was 17 when he was placed in my ninth-grade class. He had missed several years of school because he was forced to flee the genocide that took place in his country when he was only five years old. English was his second language, and Jonathan struggled to keep up with the reading and writing necessary to succeed in high school. In my classes, students are required to practice writing in a variety of genres so that they can learn to shift their style and words to match the intended audience. I try to create interesting assignments and expect the students' writing to address the given prompt. But after a few weeks, I gave up with Jonathan; regardless of the nature of the assignment, everything Jonathan wrote was about the horrors he witnessed as a child. The search for the American dream, the loss of innocence, even business letters—all centered on his heartbreak over the extermination of 800,000 people while the world looked elsewhere.

His work became impossible for me to grade—it felt ludicrous to red-ink the grammatical errors on an essay about the death of Jonathan's mother and siblings. I finally realized that this was an extraordinary young man who had endured extraordinary events, and my agenda did not meet his needs. During the time he was in my class, Jonathan continued to work on vocabulary, spelling, and grammar and usage skills, but mostly I let Jonathan just write, and I passed him on to the sophomore English teacher, who helped him gather his stories into a book. The photography teacher helped him digitize the only four photos he possessed of his childhood so that they could be used to illustrate his book.

His junior English teacher allowed him to work on a four-month research project on the history of his country to see what led to the genocide, and the history teacher helped Jonathan turn his research into a video that was shown to middle school students in the area. In his senior year, this elegant, 21-year-old man was invited to speak at his graduation ceremony, where he retold his story in heart-wrenching detail, offering his life as encouragement for those in his graduating class who felt overwhelmed by the demands of their lives and their fears of the future. Jonathan's teachers were wise enough to allow him to wander through their set curriculums so that he could harness the chaos of his life into a story worth telling and create a life worth living.

Under ordinary circumstances, we teachers need to meet our students with a plan in place that will allow us to teach and allow our students to learn. However, when we meet students with extraordinary minds or who have lived through extraordinary events, we need to be flexible enough to modify that plan. My job with Jeremy was to help him channel the flood of his extraordinary mind; my job with Jonathan was to stand back and allow his extraordinary experience to flow onto the page.

Classroom Management Tips

- Visualize a classroom setup that will allow you to teach in an environment that works to your strengths, whether it's a lecture format, small groups, or one-on-one tutoring. It may take a few years to create this environment, but if nothing else, change one thing every year.
- Well before the start of the school year, develop a clear, simple, logical classroom management plan, but be willing to modify that plan when dealing with extraordinary students or circumstances.
- Sometimes the best way to modify a student's inappropriate behavior is through stories that help the student make alternate choices when faced with life's frustrations.
- Be sure students have the sense that you know them as individuals, and not just as one of many students in your class. One of the best ways to do that is by reading their journal entries. On the next page, I've included a number of writing prompts I've used over the years that generate interesting discussions in class and provoke the students to define their values and beliefs. The first few minutes of any class can be used for journal writing while the teacher takes roll and sets up to begin the lesson (or the teacher can sit and write for five minutes at the same time). I've known math, science, history, sociology, and foreign-language teachers who have used journal writing as a way to quiet the class and get them ready to focus on the academics.

❧ Possible Prompts for Journal Entries ❧

- Is it always best to tell the truth? Why?
- When you say the word *hero*, who pops in your head? Why?
- If it comes down to it, would you choose family over friends? Why?
- Often we're at our best when those who love and know us well are proud of us, and we ourselves are comfortable in our own skin—in other words, our life works. Describe yourself at your best—how do you act, what are you doing, where are you, who are you with?
- Describe yourself at your worst—how do you act, what are you doing, where are you, who are you with?
- Joseph Campbell asks, "On what do you meditate?" Write about what you listen to or look at on the walls of your room, on television, on the computer screen.
- Quote of the Day: Do you agree or disagree with the quotation? Why?

"You train people how to treat you by how you treat yourself." (Martin Rutte)

"All that is necessary for evil to triumph is for good men to do nothing." (Edmund Burke)

"Just because you *can* do it doesn't mean you should." (Anonymous)

"People only see what they are prepared to see." (Ralph Waldo Emerson)

"The mind is its own place and in itself can make a heaven of hell, a hell of heaven." (John Milton)

"The greatest pleasure in life is doing what people say you cannot do." (Walter Bagehot)

"People seem not to see that their opinion of the world is also a confession of their character." (Ralph Waldo Emerson)

"Life shrinks or expands in proportion to one's courage." (Anais Nin)

"Goodness without knowledge is weak and feeble, yet knowledge without goodness is dangerous, and that both united form the noblest character, and lay the surest foundation of usefulness to mankind." (John Phillips)

CHAPTER 8

The Angry

Anyone can become angry—that is easy, but to be angry with the right person, to the right degree, at the right time, for the right purpose, and in the right way—that is not easy.

—ARISTOTLE

It's easy to find Rebels, Manipulators, and Victims who are angry, but the kids in this category wear their anger like a shield or deploy it like a weapon. Some of the Angry have been traumatized by physical or emotional abuse; some have suffered through a particularly difficult divorce in the family or the death of a parent or sibling. I've known others who were born with an edge; they tend to overreact to the slightest frustration and may turn to illegal substances in an attempt to find a way to function at home and at school. If their anger is out of control, a doctor may prescribe drugs to rebalance the chemicals in their brains so that these students can focus enough to participate productively in a classroom. The Angry can definitely hurt a teacher's feelings, and some look forward to a confrontation that has a built-in audience, so much of the work you do with the Angry must be done outside of the classroom.

✌ Respecting the Great Gift of Anger ✌

Terry was a junior when I first met him. He was never a student in my class, but I certainly heard of him through his reputation. His temper tantrums were legendary, and he was often called into the office because he had stormed out of a classroom or off of a playing field. Sometimes Terry was furious because a teacher gave him a demerit for being late to class; other times Terry would direct his anger at a student who was "bugging" him. But the worst fits of anger I observed happened when Terry was angry with himself because he missed a play in basketball or failed a test. In such cases, it was best to let Terry leave the class to cool down because his temper was such that he was capable of taking a swing at a teacher or anyone who tried to stop him physically from going.

When dealing with Terry, it was helpful to know his background. From the time he was a very small child, Terry's father spanked him to try to control his son's outbursts, and the spankings turned to beatings as Terry grew older. His mother didn't hit him very often, but she verbally abused him, and like the father, she increased the intensity of her abuse out of frustration and because she hoped to discover the words (or for the father, the blow) that would straighten her son out once and for all. It never occurred to his parents that Terry was using their own methods for solving problems when he screamed at a teacher or got into a fight with another student—he had been well-taught at home. Luckily for Terry, the dean of students took him under her wing and helped him to find ways to diffuse his anger before it got out of hand. The first thing she did was talk to his teachers and convince them to allow Terry to leave the classroom for a few minutes when he felt his temper heating up. Often, he would go sit in the dean's office or walk around the gym area. Terry was not free to just take off, and the dean worked out a system so that Terry had a sense of choice within the parameters of the school rules. Terry was responsible for his schoolwork, but some days, the most important lesson he learned was that there were alternate ways of releasing and reducing his anger. He didn't have to let it get the best of him.

The best advice the dean gave to Terry actually helped the boy embrace his most dominant trait. She said,

> My anger is too great a gift to give to just anyone. The only people in my life who can make me lose my temper are those people I love the most, but you allow everyone to get to you. The opposite of love is not hate—those are both very deep emotions. The opposite of love and hate is indifference. I think what it comes down to is that you just care too much about too many people.

Terry just stared at her, then said he had to go think about that for a while—she said that she could actually see his paradigm begin to shift. Under the dean's guidance, Terry began to harness his anger rather than let it take control of him, but unfortunately, he was removed from school before graduation because he lost control and attacked another student in the gym. The dean heard from him years later; living in the "real world" hadn't been an easy adjustment for Terry, but he was enrolled in college and taking courses to prepare for a career in business.

❦ Learning to Increase Your Choices ❧

I work with the Angry in my classes every year, so I purposely choose books and articles for the students to read that will generate a discussion of this emotion (see an example at the end of this chapter). I let the students know that when we lose our tempers, we also lose control. I surprise them by saying that the hardest students for a teacher to control are those students who possess self-control. Amber had been a student in my ninth- and tenth-grade English classes, and it took a while to prove to her that these statements were true. Amber was angry with her parents because they had gone through a messy divorce; she was angry with her stepmother because she felt the woman had no right to try to tell her what to do; she was angry with most of her teachers because they made her do work that she didn't enjoy; she was angry with many of her peers because they annoyed her. In fact, I can't think of a single person in her life she didn't write off in anger at one point or another. Amber was the kind of person who would say, "I'm a Scorpio and Scorpios are known for their tempers, so people just have to deal with it!" Oh, yes, she and I went round and round on a number of occasions. I would never lose my temper with her, but I was one of the few adults she had encountered in her life who wasn't impressed with her tantrums.

The main tactics I used with Amber were preparation and consistency. I would let her know well ahead of time what she was expected to do and what would happen if she didn't fulfill her responsibilities, then I would calmly enforce the consequence in as matter-of-fact a manner as possible. Amber knew how to kick up some dust, and it surprised me that so many adults in her life would give in to her. In their minds, it was easier to give her what she wanted than to deal with her rage. What they didn't know was that her tantrums would only increase, and because the adults had taught her that confrontation was a successful strategy—they would give up and release her from a consequence—Amber was rather out of control in high school. I spent a great deal of time talking with Amber and trying to understand her point of view. It's just about impossible to make any progress with the Angry unless you've taken the time to get to know them as individuals. It's also important to let them know that you like them as people, but you do not like their heated responses to frustrations.

Amber had heard every lecture imaginable about her inappropriate behaviors, so I knew I had to get her attention in another way. One day, she stormed into my classroom during lunch; she had just come from the principal's office where she had been chastised for speaking rudely to the librarian. She, of course, was innocent; she said she blew up at the librarian because the woman yelled at her to be quiet when lots of other people were talking, too. I laughed and said in mock innocence, "Gosh, I wonder why she picked on you. Oh, that's right, you and she have the same fight about once a week, right?" She snorted and shouted, "That woman is ridiculous—she hates me!"

I picked up a notebook and pretended to search for something in it, "Wait a minute, wait a minute, let me see. Ah, yes, here it is." I smiled at her. "I've been keeping a list of the people you've had run-ins with during the last week—whoa, it goes on for pages and pages." She grabbed the notebook out of my hands, "Very funny." Then I got serious and said, "If I have a fight with one person, it's very possible that it's that person's fault—even if I have a fight with a couple of other people, maybe they're jerks and I was just defending myself; but when I have a pattern of fighting over and over with a wide variety of people, well, I've got to be a big part of the problem." She started to protest, but I quickly added, "Amber, when you lose your temper, it's as if you're handing the remote control for your life to someone else. They can push the buttons at will—you shouldn't give them that much power."

I then asked her to sit down and get comfortable—it was story time. She rolled her eyes but settled in. I told her the tale of my three daughters—Delaney, Jenny, and Casey. I never spanked my kids, but I would lecture them to the point of stupefaction if they misbehaved. As they entered adolescence, I gave them a great deal of trust, but they had to fulfill their responsibilities around the house and at school. Each daughter had her own way of dealing with the work she didn't want to do. As a teenager, Delaney could be passive aggressive—when I confronted her about a problem, she quietly listened and never answered back, but in her mind, she was chanting, "I'm not going to do it." Jenny had a quick temper, and if I talked too long, World War III would break out. She inherited her temper from me—'twas the old "rock meeting the hard place" scenario. I learned to slip notes under her door that simply stated what she needed to do and what would happen if she didn't, which usually worked. Amber was laughing because she herself had responded to lectures the same as Delaney and Jenny. But she was surprised to hear that Casey was the most difficult for me to control; at a very young age, Casey intuited that when she took care of her responsibilities, people interfered less with her life. I told Amber that it was hard for me to restrict Casey because she handled herself in such a mature way at school and at home. Casey enjoyed a great deal of freedom as a teenager, to the point that it sometimes made me uncomfortable, but I had to trust her because she gave me little reason not to do so. I finished with a flourish, "So, kid, it's time for you to get all of these people out of your hair! Set yourself free! Take control of your temper and you'll take control of your life!" I wish I could have cued the national anthem just then, but she got the point.

We had many other talks over the years, and Amber made some progress, but these habits were hard for her to break and her parents never did change the way they responded to her anger, so she was still rewarded for her outbursts. Luckily, before she graduated, we were at a point where I could tease her and actually get her to laugh. She had been on a campaign to convince her parents to buy her a car as a graduation gift. When she told me they'd agreed, I wanted to say, "You're getting a car as a reward for what?" but wisely just smiled. One afternoon, she burst into my room raging over the fact that her parents wouldn't let her go out that weekend because she was failing two classes. I just listened, and when she'd calmed down, I wrote $5,000 on a Post-it note and handed it to her. She looked up puzzled, so I explained, "Put this on your mirror and whenever your parents annoy you with their unreasonable demands, just glance at this number—I figure that's how much they'll spend on that car they're buying for you. It'll help you keep things in perspective." She gave me her well-honed glare and huffed out of the room, but she understood. Years later, she still keeps in touch and has thanked me for not giving up on her. Living on her own has been a hard adjustment for Amber, but she's finding her way.

❧ Outlawing the "Board of Education" ❧

I've been teaching long enough that I actually witnessed corporal punishment before it was outlawed. I never saw it used in California, but it was still legal when I moved to Tennessee. I had just taken a job teaching in a rural high school way out in the country. The self-described "good ole boy" who taught next door, Mr. Purdy, asked me to step into the hallway with him. He said he needed a witness. I had no idea what he as talking about, but I stepped out of my classroom anyway. The teacher had pulled a very large 17-year-old boy into the hallway, and he told the boy to bend over and grab his ankles. Then, Mr. Purdy picked up a 2-foot, wooden paddle and smacked the kid hard on the rear end. The boy literally jumped a foot. Both the teacher and the student started to laugh when they turned and saw the horrified look on my face. When I walked back into my classroom, my students howled when they found out that I was upset over the way Bubba had been disciplined. This led to much teasing from students and other faculty members over the next few weeks, but I stood by my belief that physical force was the least effective form of discipline.

One day, I had a chance to prove my point. Mr. Purdy stopped me in the faculty lounge and asked if I needed him to give anyone a "couple of licks" with the paddle that day. He and a few of the other teachers started laughing, and I made myself laugh, too. Then I patted the chair next to me and said, "You'd better sit down, my friend. I'm about to expand your consciousness." I had good-naturedly taken his relentless teasing, so he was willing to play along. I asked him, "Why did you paddle Bubba the other day?"

Mr. Purdy responded, "Because he got mad and tried to punch another student."

"So you hit him to teach him not to hit someone else?"

Mr. Purdy narrowed his eyes and said, "I don't know what you people do out in California to make the kids behave, but paddling is the only thing that works with a boy like Bubba."

Then I asked, "Did Bubba's parents ever spank him?"

Mr. Purdy laughed, "Oh, yeah, he was a devil of a kid, and his daddy used to beat him just about every day."

I nodded and said, "So, he was paddled daily as a child—how often do you think he's been paddled this year in school?"

"I'd say about once a week at least—he's got a bad temper."

"So, either his parents or his teachers have paddled him on a regular basis since he was a kid, and he's still constantly in trouble? I'm thinking that "board of education" you used on him the other day isn't making much of an impression. Maybe it's time to try something else."

The other teachers in the lounge started laughing, and Mr. Purdy just shook his head and told me he took my point, but that I was a little naïve about how to handle a kid like Bubba. As it turned out, Bubba was in my vocational English class the next year, and I never had to hit him once. Mr. Purdy and I ended up becoming friends, and it was the state legislature, not me, that made him retire his paddle. In his experience, punishing Bubba that way was an effective deterrent for average students. The problem is that using physical force on a kid who resorts to physical violence when his temper is out of control teaches him the wrong lesson. That's true for any type of punishment that involves insults, humiliation, or fear; those are the tools of a bully, not an educator.

Realizing It's Not Personal

In working with the Angry, we teachers have to model how to handle our tempers in an appropriate way. It's hard to do, but a teacher cannot take something a student says in anger personally. Unless that student is your son or daughter, he or she doesn't know you well enough to truly hurt you. If a student lashes out at something I say, I don't lash back at the kid—instead, I try to think of what may have happened to provoke such a response. Unless I'm trying on purpose to make the kid mad (and in that case, it's time for me to find another profession), the student's anger is a symptom of a much deeper problem, and it would be worth my time to try to figure out what is wrong.

I remember a situation when a kid blew up in class because his teacher innocently instructed the students to ask their fathers a question that evening as part of a homework assignment. What the teacher didn't know was that the student's father had abandoned the family the week before, and the boy went home to chaos every night as his mother tried to figure out how they were going to pay the bills. The student's outburst was not a personal attack on the teacher, and it would be foolish for the teacher to take it as such.

In our classrooms, we demonstrate to the students how adults handle touchy situations, and we also insist that the students act respectfully in class. An occasional burst of temper is not a lack of respect; however, speaking rudely to a teacher on a regular basis is. Basically it comes down to treating the students as we would like to be treated. It starts with us.

Classroom Management Tips

- Do not take what students say in anger personally—try to figure out what is causing the anger.
- Respond to the students in a professional manner and model the behavior you would like them to copy.
- When it is necessary to administer a punishment, handle it in a businesslike manner—the student should know about the consequence ahead of time and view it as a reasonable response to his or her inappropriate behavior.
- Work with the administrator in charge of discipline to formulate a plan that will allow a student with a hot temper a way to cool down away from the classroom.
- The Angry are often stuck in frustrations about the past or the present, so I try to help them diffuse their resentment by focusing on the future. In the first week of school, I ask my students to list all of the careers that strike their interest from a sheet I found on the Internet that categorizes a hundred jobs by the type of work done on that job—Health, Arts/Entertainment, Business, Engineering, Law Enforcement, and so on. I tell the kids that I'm going to list their career goals on big posters that will be pinned to the wall right above the white board in the front of the class. I refer to these goals often as I teach because I want to emphasize that reading and writing skills are used in every type of job, and I learn a great deal about a kid based on the type of work he or she wants to pursue. I make sure to include one of my own goals on the poster so that the kids see that there's always something to look forward to at any stage of our lives (see example at the end of the chapter).
- Have the students read articles and books that will initiate discussions about problem solving so that the kids can discover more appropriate ways to handle their anger. Every story revolves around a conflict, so fiction is an excellent resource. For example, as part of a unit on memoir, I have my students read *This Boy's Life* by Tobias

Wolff. As a boy, the author lives for several years with Dwight, a stepfather he detests. Much later in his life, when he loses his temper with his own children, Tobias is horrified to hear Dwight's words coming out of his own mouth. On the following pages are two worksheets I use when teaching this unit; the first is designed to help the students with reading comprehension, but also generates productive discussions about how Tobias is more like Dwight than he cares to admit. The second gives the students a chance to think about a person in their own lives who is difficult for them to deal with partly because of similar personality traits (see examples on the following pages).

We Have Goals!

Pilot
Bill
Elisa

Physicians
Mason
Ethan
Raymond

Computers
Megan
Taylor

Professional Sports
Basketball:	Dan
	Josh
	Felicia
Baseball:	Doug
Soccer:	Mark
	Claire
	Austin
Paintball:	Ben
	Simon
Golf:	Kam

Musician
Linda
Joel

Politician
Brandon
Maria
Charles

Law Enforcement
Min Kee
Emma
Victor

Comedian
Susie
Will

Chef
Delaney
Jean

Dancer
Kathleen
John

Veterinarian
Sylvie

Actor/Actress
Anna
Dorothea

Teacher/Professor
Cornelia
Leigh

Writer
Cynthia
Amy
Vickie

Farmer
Beau
Barbara

Lawyer
Casey
Dick

Art/Design
Jenny
Patrick
Brian

Photographer
Richard

Singer
Cody
Trent

Librarian
Paula

Childcare
Mary
Frances

(Note: I mix all of my students from all of my classes together according to their career goals on three large poster boards. As the year progresses, students can add or cross out their names as they learn more about various jobs.)

This Boy's Life

First, list five adjectives that describe Toby's personality:

1.

2.

3.

4.

5.

Next, list five adjectives that describe Dwight's personality:

1.

2.

3.

4.

5.

Last, circle the personality traits that the two share.

In-class essay: Compare and contrast Toby's and Dwight's personalities and discuss how Toby is starting to adopt Dwight's problem-solving methods in his own life.

This Boy's/Girl's Life

List five adjectives that describe your personality:

1.

2.

3.

4.

5.

Think of someone close to you who can be difficult for you to deal with. List five adjectives to describe that person's personality:

1.

2.

3.

4.

5.

Circle the personality traits that both of you share.

In your journal, write about the similarities and differences in your personalities.

CHAPTER 9

The Invisibles

"I wanna find one face that ain't looking through me"

—FROM THE BRUCE SPRINGSTEEN
COMPOSITION ENTITLED "BADLANDS"

A couple of years ago, I mentioned a student to a colleague, and my friend had no idea as to whom I was referring—not unusual except that this boy had attended our school for four years. Every school has students who are experts at blending into the background. They quietly go about their business hoping to avoid unwanted attention from teachers and other students, but wanting recognition. They're the kids you have to look up in the yearbook a few years after graduation because you can't remember who they are, and in extreme cases, they're the kids who can cause incredible damage to themselves or to the school.

One of the reasons I work with my students in small groups is to avoid overlooking the Invisibles. Within 30 seconds of the late bell, I quickly glance around the room to take roll so I can post the names of any missing students outside the door. I'm always running out of time at the end of class, so I don't stop to call each student by name, but I have to let the front office know if anyone is missing. Early in my teaching career, someone impressed on me that during the time a student is scheduled to be in my classroom, I am legally responsible for supervising him or her. If a student cuts class and gets hurt, and I haven't told anyone that I don't know where she is, I could open myself up to a lawsuit. But I don't want to waste time calling out names—I think that's a poor beginning to a class after the first few days of school and may invite behavior problems because it can become absurdly repetitive. So I glance around, count heads, and if I'm one short, I look more carefully. I used to think I would notice if a kid was missing, but Invisibles have fooled me before. They're very, very good at disappearing, even when they're sitting right in front of you.

Offering Choices in Your Curriculum

Sometimes these kids are painfully shy, sometimes they're self-conscious, and sometimes they just want to be left alone. A teacher's job is to engage all of the students, but with Invisibles, it's a good idea to move slowly. In my current teaching situation, all students are required to participate in a schoolwide speech contest. The kids give speeches in their individual English classes, where two "winners" are chosen to compete with others at that grade level, then two representatives from each grade level compete in front of the entire school. I was not particularly shy, but as a kid, I hated public speaking; I was just self-conscious, but a speech contest is an Invisible's worst nightmare. I listened to my colleagues, who argued that learning to speak clearly and effectively in front of a group is a skill as valuable on the job as learning to write clearly and effectively. I had to agree, but when I incorporated the unit into my curriculum, I required all of my students to give a speech, but I gave them a choice as to whether or not they wanted to compete in the contest. First, I worked with the students on speech writing. Then the students had to deliver their speeches to their small groups—they had the choice of standing or sitting. I even showed them a few tricks like holding a solid book or folder so that the audience wouldn't notice their hands shaking.

Before they gave their speeches, I handed the students a rubric to give them an idea about how I would grade the speeches. In the first round, the students were fulfilling a requirement in conditions as low-risk as I could create. Then I asked for volunteers to compete for a place in the grade-level speech contest. These speeches would be delivered in an assembly room with a podium, and the other students in the class would complete an evaluation form to help choose the winners. In some classes, five or six kids were competing, in others only two or three. Before the all-school contest, I would often give a contestant a chance to practice quietly outside of the classroom by delivering the speech to an Invisible. These kids who dread having to stand in front of a group to speak can often provide very good advice on how to capture an audience's attention. By being sensitive to their fears and letting them participate in the speech exercises in a more comfortable way, I turned the contest into a learning rather than traumatizing experience for the Invisibles in my class. To my surprise, all of my students rated the speech contest as one of the most useful skills we studied on their end of the year evaluations.

Encouraging Personal Growth

The schoolwide speech contest takes place in the spring, so in the fall, I set up a number of activities that allow the kids to practice speaking in front of a group. One of the most popular is a CD I have them make of the songs of their lives; this is part of a unit of study on *The Odyssey* and the Hero's Journey. I tell the kids that songs often help us remember various stages of our lives—I know when I hear a Beach Boys song, I am right back in eleventh grade, driving over the hill to Santa Cruz with my friends. Songs bring us comfort and joy—we even send songs to our friends because the words remind us of that person or a shared experience. My students create a timeline of their life journey so far, marking the highs and lows and, in some cases, the turning points. Then they design a cover and list the songs and the artists on the back. Inside they create liner notes that explain their choices. They don't have to actually burn a CD of their songs, but many of them do—I tell them that they'll love to listen to that CD later in their lives. Their children will love it, too, and make great fun of their tastes in music.

My students attack this assignment with great enthusiasm, but some dread the last step, which is to share it with their class. To give them practice for the speeches later that year, I ask them to stand in front of the class, show the cover, read the list of songs, and share the reasons they chose a few of the songs. In the past, I've seen friendships made when classmates discover they like the same music; stereotypes are broken when the kid who's been labeled a nerd for his good grades reads a list of songs that includes Led Zeppelin, Tupac, Muddy Waters, and Nine Inch Nails. As the due date approaches, I seek out some of the extremely shy Invisibles to make sure they're OK about presenting their CDs. A student I was very concerned about one year was Randy. His father had died in a car accident when he was eight years old, and earlier that year, his mother had succumbed to cancer. He was taken in by very loving relatives, but Randy, who was a shy boy to begin with, was walking wounded that year and tried to draw as little attention to himself as possible. In thinking about him, I almost skipped the assignment, but instead, I took Randy aside to let him know that all he had to do was show his CD cover and read the titles of a few of the songs. He appreciated that—we both knew that to excuse him from giving a presentation altogether would draw far too much attention, so we created a plan where he'd look at me when he was done, and I'd interrupt with a random observation on the last musician mentioned that would turn into a rambling free association about other musicians. This would not strike my students as unusual at all. (I understand noisy minds that sometimes fire around the room like pinballs—I can truly alarm someone in a brainstorming session.)

So Randy and I had a plan, and he understood that he needed to stand in front of the class for just a minute. What actually happened took both of us by surprise. Randy walked to the front of the room with his CD in hand and stooped slightly forward so that his hair covered part of his eyes. He showed us a cleverly drawn cover that represented his passion for fantasy comics, especially those about knights on a quest. Then he read through the list of songs, and I kept waiting for him to glance at me so I'd know when to create the diversion. He never did. He opened the CD and began talking about each of the ten songs he'd chosen. It was by far the most consecutive sentences any of the students had heard him say all year. The songs were about the city of his birth, his older brother, a family vacation when he was five years old, the loss of his father, his mother's funeral, his plans for the future. The other students and I were stunned— even though it was obviously painful for him to talk, he couldn't stop, and I didn't interfere. In some ways, it was a catharsis for Randy, and his fellow students handled it beautifully.

Randy became a little more outgoing as he grew older and joined in school activities, but I think he'll always be shy. That experience allowed him to be fully visible to his peers, even for a short time, and it made a difference in how they related to him. When I was his age, I cheerfully took an F when told that I had to give a speech in front of the class. I never once had a teacher try to figure out why I was being defiant or to help me find a way to fulfill the requirement in a less threatening manner. We teachers need to be open and flexible enough to realize that, when designing our curriculum, one size does not fit all.

Dealing With Other Challenges

Not all of the Invisibles fade into the background because they are shy. Some of my quietest students are those for whom English is a second language, and they are self-conscious about speaking aloud in class. Others, possibly because they process information slowly or their vocabularies are limited, dread reading. Personally, I am delighted when someone gives me a book as a gift, but I've dealt with kids throughout my teaching career who act as if I am trying to burn their hands when I offer them a book to read. But I know students will have to grapple with the printed word throughout most of their lives, so I work to create a positive interaction with at least one book for each student, regardless of their reading levels.

Recently, I worked with a very young ninth grader from Korea, who was struggling with living in a different country, making new friends, and keeping up in her classes—all while trying to translate from Korean to English every single word she heard, spoke, or read. Mia's face fell when I announced in the second week of the school year that we'd begin reading a new book that day. I handed out *Persepolis* by Marjane Satrapi, the autobiography of a young girl living through the Islamic Revolution in Iran, and I smiled as I saw Mia's face light up when she opened the cover and discovered that it was a graphic novel—it looked like a comic book. Satrapi's story generated all sorts of discussions about living under repressive regimes and about the way the U.S. government is sometimes viewed in other countries. The pictures made the words easier to read, and Mia was able to quietly contribute what she had experienced in her life. I later discovered that Mia was a passionate artist, but rarely shared her work. A sketch she did that became the title page for her first essay about *Persepolis* and her artwork for her CD project made Mia very visible for her classmates, but on her own terms.

❧ Finding a Sense of Belonging ❧

Teachers are not responsible for making sure all of their students could compete for "most popular," but you would be wise to figure out ways to ensure that none of your students would be voted "least likely to matter to anyone." Most Invisible kids will quietly ride out their school years in one way or another, but a few will demand to be noticed. In my career, I've become aware of a handful of quiet, well-mannered teenagers who were in fact boiling caldrons of rage and resentment. I can remember giving one student a ride home and becoming frightened by his pure, unfiltered hate for his classmates. He never raised his voice or moved his hands, but he slowly and methodically described what he wanted to do to some of the "stars" of the school.

In watching him move about the campus, it never would have occurred to me that he was anything but shy. He was always willing to help when asked, earned above-average grades, and had never been in any fights with other students. Pretty much everyone ignored him, which could have been a big mistake. I talked with a teacher who seemed to have a friendly relationship with him, and that teacher went out of his way to get the boy involved in an afterschool backgammon club he was starting. Slowly, the boy began to make friends who enjoyed the same games, which relieved some of that sense of alienation. It's essential to help these kids feel like necessary members of an eclectic community. In extreme cases, children who do not feel "seen" are capable of horrendous acts to get everyone's attention.

A few years ago, I noticed that a quiet boy who ate lunch by himself every day happened to be eating a particularly good-looking chocolate cupcake. I sat down next to him and teased by saying that if he ever came to school again flaunting his chocolate right in my face, I'd put him in detention. The next day, he left a plate of chocolate cookies on my desk. He loved the attention, and it was our private joke. In fact, he started bringing me so much chocolate that I called him the "Pusher Man" and pretended to hide when I saw him coming. The other students still thought he was kind of weird, but they had a chance to see another side to his personality.

As teachers, we are asked to do so much with the little time we have, and we've all been tempted to pass by a student who needs to be seen but is not overtly demanding to be noticed. As Arthur Miller advises us in *Death of a Salesman,* "Attention must be paid."

Classroom Management Tips

- Regardless of how many years you teach, stay in touch with the fears, joys, and motivations you experienced as a kid.
- Remember that just because you enjoy doing something, doesn't mean that your students will enjoy it, too (like giving speeches or singing or playing sports). The best you can do is demonstrate why you love that activity so much, but be sensitive to students who have a way of approaching learning or life that is different from yours.
- Because they will not demand your attention, keep an eye out for the Invisible students inside and outside of your classroom, and try to find a way to involve them in activities that will make them feel like part of the community.
- Find classroom activities, such as the CD project, that will help the Invisibles reveal themselves to their peers in a situation that's as low-risk as possible (see example on the next page).
- Be aware of Invisibles who may be walking time bombs and make the school counselor or an administrator aware of your concerns. You are not saying that the student is capable of violence, just that you are concerned about his or her emotional health. A counselor can call a student in just to talk about future plans without letting the student know that you suggested the conference.

Name _____

Date Due _____

CD or Autobiography
Project for *The Odyssey*

As with Odysseus, your life has been full of twists and turns. Now you have a chance to reflect on your journey so far and illustrate it for the rest of the class. Choose one of the formats described below or come up with another format (PowerPoint, slide show, comic book, etc.) on your own. (If you decide to do something other than a CD or Autobiography, see me for a final approval.)

1. Design a cover (front and back) for a CD about the songs of your life. Be sure to write liner notes that explain your song choices.

   Or

2. Design the cover, title page, table of contents, and preface for an autobiography of your life so far. You may include illustrations or photos.

This is a writing assignment, so proofread your work carefully.

Grading Rubric:

Creativity   50 points

Thoroughness and Attention to Detail   30 points

Presentation   20 points

CHAPTER 10

The Perfectionists

Have no fear of perfection—you'll never reach it.

—SALVADOR DALI

Perfectionists put themselves under tremendous pressure to be the best. The pursuit of perfection sometimes begins with the parents, but these children often readily embrace the myth themselves. They're the ones who develop ulcers from worrying and who obsessively calculate and recalculate their GPAs. I've had students who could barely let go of an essay for fear that an undiscovered error still lurked somewhere in the shadows of the syntax. I have witnessed more than one of these students go through a nervous breakdown in the spring semester of their senior year. They can become behavior problems if they think they can challenge the teacher's methods or system of assessment—and their parents will back them fully in this attack. They're often top students, and their approach to their work tends to be rewarded with top grades, so it's sometimes difficult to help them see that their obsessive behavior is becoming a problem.

I was talking to a long-time friend the other day who has taught in elementary schools for almost 30 years. When she first began working in the 1970s, kindergarten was designed to help small children transition from home to school; most of the activities centered on socialization, language acquisition, and supervised play. Now she tells me that five-year-olds are asked to master skills that used to be introduced in second grade. Everyone wants his or her children to tap their potential as they grow up, but kindergarten used to be a place where kids could ease into that potential when they were developmentally ready. Nobody wants to see a child "left behind," but it's important to realize that school curricula increasingly rely on standardized tests as the single measure of growth and success. Anyone who has taught or raised more than one child knows that people learn in different ways and at different speeds, and when kids are pressured to master benchmarks before they're ready, their natural joy of learning is quelled.

Defusing the Tyranny of Grades

Many perfectionists enjoy the challenge of a standardized test. Most are very bright students who are good at quickly grasping which concepts are likely to be assessed, and they know how to feed that information back to the teacher. These children should feel supremely confident in their ability to excel in school, but Perfectionists are often plagued with self-doubt, and many are highly competitive. An A is not good enough—if they can't receive a perfect score, they at least demand of themselves that they receive the highest grade in the class. I can remember spending a half hour after school trying to comfort a young man who earned an A on an essay, but he was distraught because I had circled two comma errors. He begged me to erase my marks even when I pointed out that it would make no difference in his final grade—he had earned an excellent evaluation, but for him, the paper was flawed, and that was all he saw. He became increasingly agitated as we talked, but I stayed calm, explained the rule behind the placement of the commas, and tried to change the subject. I finally calmed him down by pointing out all of the "perfect" things he had done in writing his essay and letting him reprint it with the correct commas. It didn't change his grade, but it comforted him to staple the "perfect" essay to the other one in his portfolio. I'm sure this young man would be diagnosed as obsessive-compulsive, and later in his life, he would probably need all of the pens on his desk lined up in a set order before he could begin to work. His writing skills were excellent when he entered my class—that's not what he needed to work on. My job was to relieve him from the tyranny of grades. I do this with all of my students by giving many assessments that address a wide variety of skills.

Creating Tests That Are Useful

It's easy to fail a student—I know exactly how to do it. First, I would give only three or four grades for an entire grading period; second, I would give lots of grammar and usage assessments; and third, I would not allow for revision. I could invoke fear among my students and wear the mantle of "the toughest teacher on campus." I'm not sure why I would want to do this, but I have worked with colleagues who take great pride in wielding the F stamp. They feel they are the Keepers of the Standard and refuse to yield. Education is the only business I know where you can fail a large percentage of your product and still retain your job. I've talked with beginning teachers whose classes were in full rebellion because so many kids were failing; as students, these teachers had an aptitude for the subject they're now teaching and are appalled by the pathetic work their students are submitting.

I encourage all teachers to think about assessments in a different way. For one, an assessment should always be accompanied by an explanation as to why the work was excellent, very good, average, below average, or failing. I work with an outstanding math teacher who has lobbied to abolish the spring semester final exam because the students never see the corrected test and therefore no learning takes place. Next, an assessment should be an indicator of the student's progress and growth in the specific skills he or she has been studying. When faced with a class where some students are working well above grade level and others are working well below grade level, teachers must figure out how to challenge the top students without defeating those who struggle. Third, in any given subject, more than one skill is being taught. For example, in English, I am working with the students on their reading, writing, and thinking skills—each of which can be broken down into subcategories of skills: content, organization, usage, diction, and syntax, for example. I also give grades for the skills that will help my students succeed in any discipline: coming to class with all of the necessary tools, turning work in on time, and participating in a positive manner—a variety of grades properly reward the student who has a solid work ethic but is baffled by the subject matter. Teachers are hired for their talent in motivating people to succeed, not for their ability to make them fail.

Discovering the Perfect Response

One of my favorite stories to illustrate how poorly conceived assessments can backfire concerned the poet T. S. Eliot and a perfectionist named Maggie. Year after year after year, the kids in the advanced English classes were told that they had better master whichever given skill was being taught because "Mrs. Bolen will expect you to know this!" Mrs. Bolen was the last ticket to an honors diploma for these kids, and they entered her room in fear and trepidation. From the first day, the assignments were tough and required a great deal of extra work, but Mrs. Bolen took a perverse pleasure in jacking up the kids' fear as they approached the unit of study on T. S. Eliot's work. The students would read Eliot's poetry, essays, and plays, and regardless of their preparation, Mrs. Bolen told them, "Most of you will do poorly on this test. It is impossible to finish within the class period."

Several students dropped out of the class at that point. Maggie thought this whole scenario was ridiculous, but she was a top student and used to challenges. The stress level among her classmates increased as the test day drew near—this was a group of competitive kids who were used to coming out on top. They stayed up all night studying for the "impossible" test and entered Mrs. Bolen's room sick with anticipation. Maggie felt this as well, and her hands were shaking as she opened the test booklet and read the first question. She moved through the test but had trouble concentrating because "it is impossible to finish" and "you'll do poorly" kept running through her head. Maggie glanced up at one point and looked around at her classmates, most of whom were doubled over their desks in anxious poses, and without meaning to, Maggie started to giggle, softly at first, but it became louder and louder.

Her classmates shot frightened glances at her, and Mrs. Bolen glared from her desk, but Maggie could not help herself. Finally, she got up, picked up her things, and placed her test in front of her teacher. Mrs. Bolen said, "You know you will fail," and Maggie, who had probably never said a rude remark to a teacher in her life, responded, "No, Mrs. Bolen, your test is the failure." And Maggie went straight to the counselor's office and asked for a schedule change to a regular senior English class. She knew she lost her chance to become the class valedictorian, but her self-esteem mattered more to her.

I have actually sat down with a student who is obsessed with the pursuit of perfection to tell this story and describe my philosophy about grades. I refer often to a quote that hangs on the wall of my classroom: "People who never make mistakes work for people who aren't afraid to." I require all of my students to read the biography/autobiography of a person who is working in a profession in which they themselves are interested. I do this to help the kids focus on their goals as we begin our work for the school year, but I also give this assignment for the Perfectionists, because regardless of the nature of the work, all successful people experience and overcome failure. Surprisingly, some of the most difficult students teachers deal with are those who have excelled in every subject they've tackled in school.

I worked with a young lady who had received many awards for earning the highest GPA in her class from middle school on. She was brilliant, disciplined, and tenacious, and she sailed through most of the work assigned. As she moved into the advanced classes, the work became increasingly specialized and challenging, and inevitably, she received her first B on an assessment. She fell completely to pieces, and in trying to comfort her, I had to keep myself from dismissing this "tragedy"—most of the students in her class had failed the quiz. This was no comfort to her. In her mind, an above average grade was equivalent to an F. We spent a great deal of time trying to put this grade thing in perspective, and at the end of the school year, I can remember celebrating with her when she earned a C on a test in calculus—not because it was the best she could do, but because when she walked into my room, she was angry but pragmatic. She knew what she had done wrong, and she knew how to fix it. I took her out for a celebratory ice cream cone.

✥ Revealing the Secret Flaws ✥

From my first year of student teaching, I have known students who were attracted to self-destructive behaviors such as drug abuse, but the most frightening have been students who practice self-injury. Surveys have indicated that as many as one in five college students purposely hurt themselves. Some of the Perfectionists I've worked with cut or burn themselves on a regular basis. One girl told me that it was her secret flaw—her own way of escaping what she perceived to be everyone's expectations that she be perfect. I have also worked in schools where students had to withdraw just a month before graduation because the pressure they had placed on themselves to earn top grades in the most difficult classes resulted in a complete nervous breakdown.

I once walked into a study area in the back of the school library to find an outstanding scholar collapsed in a carrel, his face swollen from crying and the floor littered with papers and discarded balls of Kleenex. Andrew tried to tell me that he was fine—a perfect person would never display such behavior—but he finally confessed that he had been setting his alarm for 3 a.m. every morning so that he could study for several hours before school started. He had been operating on three or four hours of sleep a night for months, and he was at a breaking point. Andrew was also involved in a number of school and community activities in an attempt to build a stellar resume for college applications.

In talking with this student, I had to be careful not to jump right to the logical advice—your health is at risk, get more sleep. This young man planned to go to medical school and would probably need to learn to live with sleep deprivation. His parents had sacrificed a great deal to support his ambitious educational goals, and he was haunted by the fear of letting them down. It was important for me to acknowledge rather than dismiss the pressures he felt. I told him that if I ever had to undergo surgery, I would want to be in the hands of a doctor who was obsessive about wanting to get things right; but I would also want a doctor who was physically healthy enough to see me safely through the procedure. I walked with Andrew to the nurse's office and encouraged him to take the time to talk with our school counselor before he became too sick to work. He needed help to regain a sense of perspective as to how much preparation was enough, and he needed to learn that happiness is not waiting on down the road—it's part of the ride.

Explaining the Purpose of the Test

Perfectionists can be difficult for a teacher because they will argue at great length about a grade, and if they feel they're getting nowhere, some of them will not hesitate to pull a parent into the fray. A student who gets overly upset over a less than perfect grade may have learned that behavior at home. Instead of focusing on the quality of the effort a student is putting into his or her work, a parent can decide that straight A's is the sole indicator of success. I have sat through or heard about countless parent-teacher conferences where the parents have challenged what they consider to be unfair grades. It's important to let the students know exactly what you will be assessing on a particular assignment before the students begin working on it. This is one area where I envy math teachers—a problem is either computed correctly, or it's not. But an essay, ah, the ideas count for more than the format, and ideas can be tricky to assess.

I've known English teachers who give below average grades to the majority of the essays they read because, like the majority of working adults, most students cannot achieve perfection in their command of the language. I've also known teachers who give most of their students B's or C's—too many A's is suspect, and D's and F's bring in the parents. My best tools for helping a Perfectionist (and his or her parents) live with the grades I assign are (1) a portfolio that traces growth rather than consistent accuracy and (2) a rubric for each assignment that shows the specific skills I will be evaluating and the percentage of the total grade each of those skills will represent (an example is at the end of the chapter). Ultimately, I need to have clear documentation for my grades, and I need the students and their parents to believe that I have their children's best interests at heart.

&ε Asking Too Many Questions ≥&

One final piece of advice for working with Perfectionists in your classroom: These kids tend to be nervous about any upcoming assignment and want to be sure that they fully understand all possible contingencies before they begin. In short, they can radically disrupt the flow of a lesson by asking too many questions. This can cause behavior problems in the classroom because it annoys the other students (who may be a little bitter about the Perfectionists' flawless grades anyway), and it can make even the most patient of teachers respond rudely to these interruptions. Perfectionists are often very intelligent, and the minute you begin to introduce an assignment, their minds fly ahead as they rush to predict the possible pitfalls. Their hands shoot up in the air before you've had a chance to finish your explanation. When I'm getting my students ready to tackle a project, I'm also trying to sell it—I want them to be excited about spending their time exploring this new topic. Pacing is everything, and I want the anticipation to build, but a Perfectionist can break the flow by jumping ahead with his or her worries. What I've learned to do is to tell the students that I'm going to take some time to describe a project, that I've thought carefully about all of the steps it will take to complete the project, and that I'll make sure that everyone understands fully what to do before the class is over. I then tell the kids to take out a piece of scratch paper so that they can write down their questions as they occur—I ask them to give me the chance to explain what we'll be doing, then when I'm finished, I'll be more than happy to answer each and every question. What I find is that the Perfectionists are afraid they'll forget what they were going to ask, so if they're not allowed to interrupt, they focus on remembering the question and miss the explanation. Writing down the question allows them to let it go for a while, and more often than not, they find that it's been answered by the end. If I haven't addressed it, I surely want them to ask—that helps everyone.

As a kid, I was certainly not plagued by a need for perfection, but I have driven myself crazy by obsessing over a social blunder or a problem poorly solved. Obsessive behaviors are not generated on purpose—they're powerful compulsions that will demand attention. Just as it's foolish to tell an anxious person simply not to worry, it's not helpful to tell a Perfectionist to just relax. Mostly they need to talk through their stress and be given permission to be less than perfect. I tell them it's like the Navajo rug, where a slight imperfection is woven into the pattern so that the gods will not be offended. The first glimmer of understanding I got from a Perfectionist who had to be the best in class, on the athletic field, and in every activity was when I told her that the problem in her quest for perfection was that it took away the chance for anyone else to feel what she feels in that moment of glory. She understood that perfectly.

✑ **Classroom Management Tips** ✑

- Help the students understand that a grade is one teacher's evaluation of specific skills in specific circumstances at a specific moment. They are students, not A students or F students.
- Be sensitive to the pressured child when demanding excellence from your students. You should encourage the kids to push themselves, but excellence can manifest itself in different ways for different students.
- Give lots of grades so the students have many chances to succeed.
- Document your grading system so parents and students understand specifically what an A or an F will look like.
- Do not try to cure students of perfectionism; help them learn to cope with that strength, which is also a weakness.
- Give your students a rubric before they begin an assignment so that they can see exactly how you will assess their work (see example on the next page).

Name _____

Period _____

❧ Timed Writing Rubric ❧

	Possible Points	Actual Points
Effective introduction	5	_____
Clear thesis statement	10	_____
Effective organization	15	_____
Clear transitions	10	_____
Effective use of supporting details	25	_____
Effective conclusion	5	_____
Essay addresses prompt	10	_____
Few errors in grammar and usage (a clear command of the language)	20	_____
Total:	100	_____

Comments:

Before You Finish . . .

The paradox that faces education is that human beings are both similar and different.

—RENATE AND GEOFFREY CAINE

I read somewhere that schools are one of the few industries where a Rip Van Winkle, who had been asleep for 100 years, could walk through a classroom door and know exactly where he was. We have all been students at one time or another in our lives, and we tend to be rather familiar with a wide variety of teaching styles. Our students are no different—at the end of the first day of school, kids stand around exchanging stories about the "cool" teacher, the "mean" teacher, the "crazy" teacher, the "tough" teacher, the "pushover," and so on. We scan a room full of faces on the first day and try to avoid mistakes by making educated guesses as to which classroom management techniques will work best with students we barely know. Sometimes we're right, and sometimes we're wrong, but it's essential to give the kids the impression on the very first day that we have an agenda, that the agenda is designed to help them reach their goals, and that we will do what is necessary to protect the positive learning atmosphere we've set up in our classrooms. Misunderstandings will occur, but because we see our students every day, we always have the chance to clear things up.

On the second day of this current school year, my students participated in the "Assumptions" activity I described in Chapter 3. In three of my four freshman English classes, the students joined in eagerly and seemed to truly enjoy getting to know a classmate who had been a stranger the day before. However, things did not go so smoothly in my last class—maybe because it was at the end of the day, maybe because I was tired, maybe because of the mix of personalities—who knows? At any rate, as I handed out the Assumptions questions and assigned each student a partner, two boys began to snicker when I told one of them that he would be paired up with a rather attractive girl across the room. My instincts told me that Adam was just being self-conscious because Gina was good-looking, but he and his friend wouldn't stop. At one point, I heard Adam's friend say, "You're not going to write that!" and they both burst out laughing. I glanced over at Gina, and she looked down at her desk hurt and angry. I immediately took action and let the two boys know in no uncertain terms that their behavior was unacceptable and made them stay after class to talk with me.

I kept a rather tight rein on that group for a couple of days. At the end of the first week, another teacher stopped me to ask what had happened. He had been sitting around talking with several of the students from that class, and when my name came up, the teacher said, "Oh, Ms. Gill's nice, isn't she?" Adam immediately responded, "No, she's intense!" and the others agreed. Later in the year, the kids in that class told me that I was "so different" from what they first thought I'd be like as a teacher. Again, thank heavens, I see them every day. I told Adam that I made some incorrect assumptions about him, too. After two weeks, I discovered he was actually a thoughtful young man who took his work seriously, but that was not the impression I had of him based on the first few days of school.

In this book, I've described 10 general student types—not to label or stereotype kids but to look for patterns of behavior that offer clues as to how to best approach individual students when problems arise. In general, teachers set up rules, consequences, and activities that help to create a safe, friendly atmosphere in their classroom, which will increase the amount of time teachers can teach and students can learn. In their influential book *Making Connections: Teaching and the Human Brain*, Renata and Geoffrey Caine describe an optimal state of learning, which they call "relaxed alertness." This happens when teachers understand that students like the Angry or the Misfits cannot effectively participate in the lessons presented when their mind states are fear, alarm, or terror.

By understanding the archetypes presented in this book, you may learn that the most effective disciplinary technique to use with a Rebel like Commie is to give him a sense of control and choice. In the same manner, Invisibles need a sense of being recognized, and Manipulators need a project that helps rather than harms. When devising a system of classroom management, you must have a general plan that will help as many of your students as possible perceive themselves as "Good" kids, but you would be wise to approach the minority who cause serious disturbances in your classrooms with alternate disciplinary techniques, many of which will take place outside of the classroom. The most important impression you need to leave with your students is that you "get" them—you recognize them for who they are, understand their motivations, and have a sincere desire to help them bring out the best in themselves.

⧼ Listening to the Students ⧽

Last year, the yearbook staff asked all of the seniors to bring in a baby photo of themselves, then the staff created a collage and challenged the readers to try to guess which baby photo matched which senior. Most people thought the test was fun, but those photographs brought tears to my eyes. Without exception, each picture presented a sweet, innocent, trusting face; some looked much the same at age 18, but a few had changed so profoundly as to cause gasps of amazement when the match was revealed. When I am frustrated with the behavior of some truly difficult students in my class, I try to remember that they are basically good kids who have developed some rather powerful defense mechanisms that have helped them survive their childhoods. My job is to create a classroom where they feel comfortable and accepted.

It took years and years of trial and error for me to develop the specific classroom management tips that I've offered in this book. I've had the privilege of observing gifted teachers, and I've been observed myself by department chairs and administrators who have offered advice that has helped me to grow in my craft. But my best critics are my students—who else will know better what worked or didn't work in my class? At the end of each semester, I ask my students to complete an evaluation form to let me know which activities were helpful and which felt like a waste of time (an example is at the end of this chapter). I tell them that what they write on the evaluation will not affect their grade—in fact, I don't read the evaluations until the final grades have been submitted to the registrar. The kids have been in my class for several months by the end of the first semester, and most trust me enough to give me their honest opinions. These evaluations often surprise me; when I first started, I expected the kids to say that they hated the time we spent practicing spelling and grammatical rules, but that was not necessarily so. I've also had incidences where a significant number of students have told me that an activity that I found particularly enjoyable needed to be cut. I appreciate their candor and am influenced by their suggestions.

Before I lock up my room for the summer, I sit down and list all of the activities and routines that worked well and write down the things that gave me problems. Every year I fine-tune my lessons, rules, and consequences based on my students' end-of-the-semester evaluations and my own reflections. Something we have in common with our students is that we were kids ourselves. Remembering what that feels like is a great place to start.

Each day as I sat down to work on this book, I would conjure up students from my past to think about what I learned from them and what they learned from me. Sometimes I had five or six students swirling around in my head and found it to be a most pleasant way to spend my mornings. I would guess that I've taught more than 3,000 students in my career, and I wish I remembered them all, but I don't. A few have stuck in my head because their struggles to find their way were particularly painful, frustrating, or exhilarating. As in myths, they have become archetypes that I can use to help next year's students understand their own behaviors and how to fit in to the school community in healthy, productive ways. I hope their stories will offer you the same insight and inspiration that they have given to me.

English 9—Fall Semester Evaluation

Listed on the back of this page are many of the skills we practiced during the first semester. In your opinion, which activities were most **useful**?

In your opinion, which activities were **less effective**?

Other suggestions:

❧ **Fall Semester** ❧

Reading:

Biography/autobiography

Persepolis

This Boy's Life

The Glass Menagerie

Supplemental reading

Study Skills:

Annotations/highlighting the text

Character sheets

Themes/literary terms worksheets

Organization (binder checks)

Grammar and usage

Spelling demons

Creative projects (wish books, CD project)

Vocabulary

Reading techniques (SWBS charts, summaries, story maps,
think-aloud)

Test-taking strategies

Writing:

SAT prep (in-class, timed writing)

Journals

Portfolios (writing conferences)

Grammar checklist (tally sheets for errors in essays)

Research papers

Controversial issue essays

Life Skills:

Assumptions

Working cooperatively with others

False power versus true power

Transactional analysis

Goal making

Thank you for helping me improve my classes—Ms. Gill

English 9—Spring Semester Evaluation

Listed on the back of this page are many of the skills we practiced during the second semester. In your opinion, which activities were most **useful**?

In your opinion, which activities were **less effective**?

Other suggestions:

✌ **Spring Semester** ✌

Reading:

Greek Gods and Goddesses

The Odyssey

Haroun and the Sea of Stories

Supplemental reading

Study Skills:

Annotations/highlighting the text

Character sheets

Themes worksheets

Creative projects (poetry chapbook, personal myths)

Vocabulary

PSAT preparation

MLA formatting

Writing:

Business writing (letters, resumes)

Technical writing (writing and following directions)

Timed writing

Journals

Portfolios (writing conferences)

Literary analysis essays

Personal statement

Speeches

Life Skills:

On-the-job writing sample

Job interviews

The hero's journey

Problem solving

Thank you, have a wonderful summer!—Ms. Gill

Bibliography

Berne, E. (1961). *Transactional analysis in psychotherapy: A systematic individual and social psychiatry.* New York: Grove Press.

Berne, E. (1964). *Games people play: The psychology of human relationships.* New York: Grove Press.

Caine, R., & Caine, G. (1991). *Making connections: Teaching and the human brain.* Alexandria, VA: Association for Supervision and Curriculum Development.

Ernst, K. (1972). *Games students play (and what to do about them).* Millbrae, CA: Celestial Arts.

Jensen, E. (2000). *Brain-based learning: The new science of teaching and training* (Revised ed.). Thousand Oaks, CA: Corwin Press.

Kilbourne, J., & Koehmstedt, S. (1997). *Looking beyond expectations.* Oracle, AZ: Birdworks.

Levendron, S. (1998). *Cutting: Understanding and overcoming self-mutilation.* New York: Norton.

Macrorie, K. (1970). *Uptaught.* New York: Hayden Book.

Parini, J. (2005). *The art of teaching.* Oxford, UK: University Press.

Rosenblum-Lowden, R. (2000). *You have to go to school—you're the teacher!* Thousand Oaks, CA: Corwin Press.

Sizer, T., & Sizer, N. (1999). *The students are watching.* Boston: Beacon Press.

Stern, D. (1995). *Teaching English so it matters.* Thousand Oaks, CA: Corwin Press.

Walsh, D. (2004). *Why do they act that way? A survival guide to the adolescent brain for you and your teen.* New York: Simon & Schuster.

Ward, C. (2006). *How writers grow: A guide for middle school teachers.* Portsmouth, NH: Heinemann.

Wormeli, R. (2006). *Fair isn't always equal: Assessing and grading in the differentiated classroom.* Portland, ME: Stenhouse.

Young, S. (2002). *Great failures of the extremely successful.* Los Angeles: Tallfellow Press.

Zemelman, S., & Daniels, H. (1988). *A community of writers.* Portsmouth, NH: Heinemann.